3/5

The Boy Who Was Bullied

the story about the life of

John Peters Humphrey

Drafter of the
United Nations Universal Declaration of Human Rights

Anne Huestis Scott

First printing August 2011
Second printing September 2012

Editing: Grayce Rogers
Design: Anne Huestis Scott
Cover design and image prep: Brenda Conroy
Cover images:
  Front cover, Six-year-old John: Humphrey Family Scrapbook
          United Nations Emblem: UN Archives, 170728 (detail)
  Back cover, Adult John Humphrey: Walt Malone
Printed and bound in Canada

Glen Margaret Publishing
P.O. Box 3087
Tantallon, Nova Scotia B3Z 4G9
Tel 902-823-1198 fax 902-823-1928
www.glenmargaret.com

Library and Archives Canada Cataloguing in Publication

Scott, Anne Huestis, 1945-
The boy who was bullied / Anne Huestis Scott.

ISBN 978-1-897462-21-8

1. Humphrey, John P.   2. United Nations. General Assembly.
Universal Declaration of Human Rights.   3. Lawyers--Canada--
Biography--Juvenile literature.   4. Diplomats--Canada--Biography--
Juvenile literature.   5. Human rights--History--Juvenile literature.
6. Bullying--Juvenile literature.   I. Title.

FC601.H86S26 2011   j341.4'8092   C2011-905260-1

*In acknowledgement of
our son Steven, and in memory of our son Jamie,
both of whom repeatedly had their human rights abused
before we adopted them at ages three and five.*

Acknowledgements

I'm beginning to believe it takes a village to write a book!
Writing *The Boy Who Was Bullied* has been a fascinating two-
year journey. There are many who helped me along the way.

Thank you to my daughter, Heather Scott, for her dedicated
assistance in editing; and to my granddaughter Meelahn, who gave
honest reflections from a young person's point of view.

For reading the draft and making helpful suggestions, I wish
to thank: Jean Murray, my daughter Janet Scott and son-in-law
Mark Leger, son-in-law Richard Jones, Pip Murphy, the late John
Murphy, Donna Veniot, Mark Perry, George Fry, Janet and Ken
Millar, Marcia Barss, Kathy Hooper, Ida MacPherson, Mary
Naigle, Sheila Murray, Maria Machum, Carole Wallace, Teena
Foster and her Grade 6 class at Hampton Middle School,
Dr. Stephanie Inglis and Sister Dorothy Moore.

This book would not have happened without the support of
John Hobbins, retired law librarian at McGill University, who
provided me with historical information on John Humphrey; and
Guy and Martha Humphrey who loaned me the very valuable
Humphrey family scrapbooks.

I am indebted to my late 93-year-old mother, Grace Huestis,
who was a valuable source of information concerning how
everyday life used to be. (My mother suffered a stroke and died
just days after I sent my book to the publisher. She often
wondered why it was taking me two years to write a book!)

Thank you to Moni and Ernie Kuechmeister for their tour of
John Humphrey's cottage in Prince Edward Island and sharing
personal stories of Moni's stepfather, John. Thank you to John's
stepdaughter, Dorothy Malone Petersen, who affirmed John's
strong desire for children to learn about human rights, and
shared with me, John's last public words before he died.

Research was made much easier with the help of: David
Keirstead, local historian; Muriel Mealey, former Hampton
Village resident; Faye Pearson, Arthur Keith and summer
student Alex Donovan, at the Kings County Museum; Theresa
Rowat and Mary Houde at McGill University Archives; Janet
Bishop at New Brunswick Museum Archives; Nic Carhart at
Rothesay Netherwood School; Julia Thompson at Provincial
Archives of New Brunswick; Rhianna Edwards at Mount Allison
University Archives; and Veena at United Nations Archives.

Gathering over 160 images is not easy! Thank you to the following who so graciously helped me: Harold Wright, Robert McInnes, Susan Kelly, Ruth Thomson, Carolyn Hawthorne, Bill Preeper, Janet Millar, Walter Malone, Beverley Lyons, Sue Hooper, Phyllis Holmes, the late John Murphy, Judi and Glen Baxter, Marilyn and Jim McKenzie. I also want to thank the parents of toddler Jack Neil Scott Leger and infant Oakley Joseph Murphy, for allowing me to take photos of their children. A special thank you to youth artist Owen Preeper for his illustrations.

Children and teens of Hampton, New Brunswick, on the lawn of the Kings County Courthouse, beside the John Peters Humphrey sculpture.

Thank you to Carol Goodman and Heather Scott for taking photos of the skit scenes, and to the children and teens who participated, including: Grace and Joe Albert, Fahim Azimi, Bailey Barton, Emily Carlson, Amelia and Matthew Cromwell, Gabriel Della Valle, Ben Gesner, Emily J.A. and Patrick Kelly, Liam, Emily R. and Michaela Kelly, Sophie McTiernan Gamble, Chandler MacKenzie, J.D. and Rayanne McKenzie, Shaqayeq Mezbani, Owen Preeper, Connor Rennick, Stuart Ryan, Grace and Katie Ryder, Ahreeyahn and Meelahn Scott-Weabury, Brad Trecartin, Emma and Laurel Walker.

I appreciate the insightful suggestions of Kathleen Martin at The Canadian Children's Book Centre.

I also wish to thank the Hampton John Peters Humphrey Foundation, and my brother and sister-in-law, David and Faye Huestis for their financial support. With their assistance, children will be able to learn about John Peters Humphrey and Human Rights.

Throughout the writing of this book, I have felt the presence of my life-partner, the late Neil Scott, who always encouraged me and provided me with the space to create and be my own person.

Contents

Appendix   *[Educational Resource]*

Children at the John Peters Humphrey sculpture in Hampton, New Brunswick, listen as the author reads *The Boy Who Was Bullied*. Sculpture: front view of John Humphrey, the boy; back view of John Humphrey, the adult. The two figures are joined at the left shoulders, indicating the missing left arm.

Prologue

During World War II, while some children around the world lived in fear, others played happily.

From 1939 to 1945, many children around the world were playing games and having fun. Children in parts of Europe and Asia, however, were living fearfully in the midst of World War Two. An estimated sixty million people died during this war. Sixty million (60,000,000) is a very large number... too large to imagine; but let's try.

Over a six-year period, 60,000,000 people died.
   That means approximately:
      10,000,000 people died each year,
         27,000 people died each day,
            1,000 people died each hour, and
             500 people died each half-hour.

   Think of a school with 500 students. During the War, an average of this many people died each half-hour of every day and every night, for six years. Something needed to be done so that this would never happen again!

Not long after World War Two ended, world leaders from fifty countries met together. They wanted to find a way to maintain world peace and protect human rights. After much discussion, the leaders agreed to form the United Nations (UN) – hoping that this organization would result in countries talking through problems, rather than fighting. The headquarters for the UN was built in New York City.

(Front, l-r,) Henri Laugier (France), Eleanor Roosevelt (United States), John Humphrey (Canada), Charles Malik (Lebanon).

On December 10th, 1948, the UN adopted the *Universal Declaration of Human Rights* – a list of rules stating how individual human beings should be protected and respected. Originally written in English, *The Declaration* has been translated into more than 300 languages. It is still considered to be one of the most important documents ever written!

The Declaration is a lengthy document, consisting of thirty articles, based on the following rights:

The Universal Declaration of Human Rights

1. Right to Equality
2. Freedom from Discrimination
3. Right to Life, Liberty, Personal Security
4. Freedom from Slavery
5. Freedom from Torture, Degrading Treatment
6. Right to Recognition as a Person before the Law
7. Right to Equality before the Law
8. Right to Remedy by Competent Tribunal
9. Freedom from Arbitrary Arrest, Exile
10. Right to Fair Public Hearing
11. Right to be considered Innocent until proven Guilty
12. Freedom from Interference with Privacy, Family, Home and Correspondence
13. Right to free movement in and out of the Country
14. Right to Asylum in other countries from Persecution
15. Right to a Nationality and Freedom to Change it
16. Right to Marriage and Family
17. Right to Own Property
18. Freedom of Belief and Religion
19. Freedom of Opinion and Information
20. Right to Peaceful Assembly and Association
21. Right to participate in Government and in Free Elections
22. Right to Social Security
23. Right to Desirable Work and to join Trade Unions
24. Right to Rest and Leisure
25. Right to Adequate Living Standards
26. Right to Education
27. Right to Participate in the Cultural Life of Community
28. Right to Social Order assuring Human Rights
29. Community Duties essential to Free and Full Development
30. Freedom from State or Personal Interference in the above rights

Who was given the job of writing this important Declaration? Who spent months creating the first draft? Until 1988, forty years after *The Declaration* was adopted, most people didn't know whose ideas led to the creation of *The Declaration*. John Hobbins, Law Librarian at McGill University, discovered the truth when he stumbled upon hand-written documents in a filing cabinet. He quickly learned that Canadian John Humphrey was the creator, the overlooked hero.

"I do not particularly want people to remember me," Professor Humphrey stated in a video produced about his career. "I do, however, want people to remember what we accomplished with the creation of international law (a result of *The Declaration*)."

Who was Professor Humphrey, the man who worked so hard to protect the rights of others, without seeking fame for himself?

John Humphrey was an ordinary boy, born in a small Canadian town, in 1905. Young John was smart and loved to have fun. Full of mischief, John was always ready for an exciting escapade.

As a result of tragic personal loss, young John became a victim of bullying. Strong-willed, John learned to fight back, with a temper he often had difficulty controlling.

Canadian postage stamp, 1998.

When John was an adult, he became aware of international bullying. Instead of using his fist, John used his pen to stop bullies. As the first Director of the United Nations Human-Rights Division, John worked tirelessly improving individual rights and freedoms around the world.

This is the story of human rights champion, John Peters Humphrey – the man who considered his life to be "an adventure"!

Introduction to

John's Hometown and Family

John Humphrey was born in Hampton, New Brunswick, over one hundred years ago. Hampton was similar to other small towns in Canada and the United States, with a strong sense of community. The town folk all knew each other and would help one another in times of trouble. And whenever children were into mischief, their parents were sure to find out! Growing up in Hampton meant that you knew every rock, bush, path, and brook, who lived in each house, the best hiding places for hide-and-seek, and when the next train was due at the station – the railway being a never-ending attraction.

During John's childhood, Hampton consisted of two separate communities: HAMPTON VILLAGE and HAMPTON STATION.

HAMPTON VILLAGE, located beside the Kennebecasis River, was a main transportation route in the early 1900s.

View of Hampton Village, early 1900s.

Flewwelling's Lumber Mill: the mill workers cut and trimmed pine logs into match-size pieces, then packed them in wooden crates and carried them across the yard to the Match Factory.

Many who lived in the Village had family members who worked at either Flewwelling's Lumber Mill or Flewwelling's Match Factory, located next to the river.

One of the families who lived in Hampton Village was the Mabee family. Arnold Mabee was captain of the riverboat.

Captain Mabee and family: the Mabee home was located beside the Agricultural Hall (present-day Legion).

The *Steamship Clifton,* docked at the wharf in Hampton Village. The *SS Clifton* was destroyed by fire in 1905 and replaced the next spring by the *SS Hampton.*

Three times a week, for as long as the river was free of ice, the *Steamship Hampton* travelled to Hampton – the furthest stop inland on the Kennebecasis River. The riverboat sailed from the port city of Saint John, carrying freight such as lumber and large bags of feed. These were dropped off at various wharves along the river.

The *SS Hampton* was capable of holding three hundred passengers. For eighty cents, passengers could travel by riverboat, from Saint John to Hampton, and then return to Saint John by train.

HAMPTON STATION, where John's family lived, was two kilometers from Hampton Village. Built beside the rail line, Hampton Station bordered a marsh called Ossekeag Creek.

Ossekeag is a Mi'kmaq name meaning 'little marsh'. After the snow melted in the spring, the creek looked more like a lake than a marsh.

On the edge of Ossekeag Creek was the Ossekeag Stamping Factory, which made enamel pots and pans. The factory (far left) employed about 250 men.

View of Hampton Station, early 1900s.

A busy industrial community, Hampton Station had a tannery where local farmers brought cowhide to be cured and made into leather, and a blacksmith shop where iron was made into horseshoes. The blacksmith shop was also the meeting place of the local archers, who practised target-shooting with crossbows. In 1903, tennis courts were laid out between the main street and the railway station.

l-r, Tannery, Blacksmith Shop, Atheneum (General Store), Post Office (attached to the store).

In Hampton Station, there was a carriage factory where horse-drawn carriages were built. There were also a few general stores, churches and hotels.

Horse and carriage on Front Street (now Main Street).

The Atheneum, General Store owned by Robert Smith.

Barnes' Store (red-brick building), which housed a General Store and the local Telegraph Office.

Hampton Methodist Church, later known as Hampton United Church.

Wayside Inn, located beside the railway tracks.

Two doctors had their practice in the community. In case of emergency, Hampton Station had an ambulance.

Dr. J. Newton Smith

Dr. F.H. Wetmore

Hampton Station ambulance.

When the railway was built in 1859, Hampton Station grew from a place of little importance to become (in 1871) the shire town, or capital, of Kings County.

The County Courthouse was located in Hampton Station.

Kings County Courthouse

Steam-engine train

Hampton Railway Station, early 1900s.

Built in 1867, the railway station became a busy and popular meeting place with as many as ten steam-engine trains travelling through every day. The main floor of the station had a waiting room and a ticket office. The other two floors were occupied by the station master and his family.

The Humphrey House was three houses away from the railway station. It was on a large property with flower and vegetable gardens, and an apple orchard. Just behind the house, a steep slope (great for sliding in winter) dropped off to Ossekeag Creek.

Both children and adults in Hampton Station loved to skate on the creek in the winter and fish there in the spring. By summer, most of the water had drained from Ossekeag Creek into the Kennebecasis River. A small stream a few meters wide, remained, bordered by green reeds and marsh hay.

The Humphrey House

Frank Humphrey   Nellie (Peters) Humphrey

The Humphrey Children: Ruth, age 3; Doug, age 2; 1902.
(This photo was taken before John's birth, in 1905.)

Nellie and Frank Humphrey lived with their children in the Humphrey House on Railway Avenue. Frank [Papa] worked in Saint John in the family shoe business, which he had inherited from his father. Like other businessmen of the day, Frank travelled back and forth to Saint John for work, a one-hour commute by train. Like most mothers in the early 1900s, Nellie [Mama] stayed home to bring up their children.

John's Relatives

John had many relatives, some of whom played an important role in his life. Perhaps the most significant was his grandfather, Thomas Peters.

First Stock Certificate for Hampton Rural Cemetery, 1884.

GRANDPA PETERS (Mama's father) was involved in local and provincial affairs. For twelve years, he was Deputy Commissioner of Agriculture for the province.

Grandpa was keenly interested in the Hampton Rural Cemetery. For many years he was the cemetery's president, treasurer, and groundskeeper. Grandpa was proud to say he'd been issued the first stock certificate for the cemetery.

John's Grandmother Peters had died long before John was born. Grandpa remarried but the marriage didn't last long.

"She thought **he** had money and he thought **she** had money. They were both disappointed!" Mama once told the children.

After the marriage break-up, Grandpa moved in with John and his family. Grandpa rarely showed any love toward John. As a result, John wasn't very fond of his grandfather. When he grew up, John dropped the Thomas from his name.

Grandpa was a colourful, outspoken character. For John, he was the male authority in the family – a power never to be questioned!

Uncle Ralph March

John's AUNT BESSIE (Mama's sister) and UNCLE RALPH lived three houses away, on Railway Avenue. Nellie and Bessie sometimes joked about the fact that their father, Grandpa Peters, had given them cows' names. (In those days, farmers named their cows; Nellie and Bessie were two popular choices.) Aunt Bessie and Uncle Ralph's son, Ralph, was the same age as John. During their growing-up years, COUSIN RALPH MARCH, was John's favourite playmate.

John's UNCLE LEONARD (Mama's brother, who never married) lived in Saint John but often came on the train to visit. Having no children of his own, Uncle Leonard loved to spoil his nieces and nephews. He was a favourite of John's. John was proud that his Uncle Len was a soldier.

Uncle Leonard Peters

John's father's family. l-r, back row: Percy, Ralph, Guy; front row: Harry, Edith (Killam), Frank (John's father).

John's UNCLE PERCY (Papa's brother) and AUNT NELL lived in Saint John. They had a summer home on the St. John River at Ononette (now part of Grand Bay-Westfield). As a teenager, John spent many happy times with them.

John's UNCLE GUY (Papa's brother) had a shop next door to Uncle Percy's home on Orange Street, where he roasted and sold, what most town folk agreed, was "the best coffee in the province".

Uncle Percy and Aunt Nell's son, COUSIN JACK HUMPHREY, was four years older than John. As a child, John saw him as a hero – like an older brother. Jack grew up to be a well-known Canadian artist. As adults, John and Jack became good friends.

Cousin Jack Humphrey

The town of Hampton was very important to John throughout his life. Although he lived for many years in Montreal and also in New York City, John always thought of Hampton as his home. When he was an adult, working at the United Nations, John wrote in his diary:

It is strange how when unoccupied, my mind tends to fix itself on some event or scene connected with Hampton. Thus, tonight at dinner [in France], I happened to look at a picture on the wall which contained amongst other things, a rowing boat. My mind began to picture 'the boat' at Hampton and a whole series of other pictures connected with Hampton came up. And when I dream [no matter what about] the background is always Hampton.

John Humphrey, world traveller.

A row boat.

Chapter 1

The Doctor's Big Black Bag

It was an early spring evening in 1905, at the home of Frank and Nellie Humphrey, in Hampton, New Brunswick. Six-year-old Ruth marched around the kitchen carrying her Eaton's Beauty Doll. Her younger brother Doug, age five, led the way around the table and past the wood stove, shouting, "Hup-2-3-4, hup-2-3-4…"

With arms swinging wide, Doug started singing, "*The grand old Duke of York, he had ten thousand men. He marched them up to the top of the hill and he marched them down again!*"

"Follow me, Ruth!" Doug directed, as he jumped up on the couch.

"I'm not jumping on the couch," Ruth replied. "I don't want to drop Dolly. Her china head might crack open."

"**At-ten-tion**! Soldiers dismissed!" Doug shouted.

An Eaton's Beauty Doll was every little girl's dream.

Ruth carried her doll over to the small wooden cradle Papa had bought for her. Doug got out his box of tin soldiers and played by himself.

While the children played, Nellie brought in wood from the woodshed. Frank was out in the barn checking on the ponies. Returning to the house, he saw Nellie carrying an armload of wood.

"Nellie," said Papa, in a hushed voice, "you shouldn't be carrying that! It's too heavy for you in your delicate condition."

Ruth was delighted with the doll's cradle that Papa had bought for her.

Doug lined up his tin soldiers.

Mama wanted to help with some of the heavier chores. She knew that Papa was feeling weak from the cancer he had been battling for over a year. Papa had been very ill six months ago. He had spent two long months at the hospital in Montreal receiving treatment.

"Frank," Mama quietly but firmly responded, "I don't think the baby will arrive for a few weeks. I'll be careful."

Doug was busy lining up his tin soldiers, but had overheard the conversation.

"What baby?" he puzzled.

Ruth jumped excitedly to her feet. "Mama, are we getting a baby?!"

Mama blushed, "Why yes, Ruth."

Ruth danced around, singing, "We're going to get a new baby!"

"I hope it will be a baby boy!" Doug beamed.

Ruth suddenly frowned. "When will the doctor bring us a baby?"

"Before summer," Mama said shyly, looking over at Papa.

"How?" questioned Doug.

Ruth had heard a girl at school talking about her new baby cousin. She knew how it happened.

"The doctor brings the baby in his big black doctor's bag, of course!" Ruth announced.

The doctor's big black bag.

Chapter 2

Sunday Surprise

Hampton Methodist Church, which John's family attended on Sunday mornings.

"Why is Papa always taking naps?" wondered Ruth, as she gazed at her father asleep on the couch.

Papa stirred from his sleep and opened his eyes to see Ruth staring at him.

"Ah, Ruth," Papa yawned, "you must be wondering about your sleepy papa. Well, on Friday I'll be taking the train to Montreal. I have an appointment on Saturday morning at the hospital, with a specialist." Papa stretched and yawned again. "I'm hoping the doctor will help me feel better soon. I might have to stay a few weeks for treatments," Papa winked, "but then I'll be back."

On Sunday, April 30th, the weather was sunny and cool. When Ruth and Doug woke up, they got dressed in their best clothes. The Humphrey family went to church on Sunday mornings; Mama sang in the choir.

Mama's sister, Aunt Bessie, was downstairs in the kitchen preparing breakfast. She often dropped in, although not usually this early in the morning. Uncle Ralph was beside the wood stove polishing Doug's boots when Ruth and Doug arrived in the kitchen.

"Where's Mama?" the children asked.

"Mama's not feeling well," Aunt Bessie answered, as she served up porridge in their bowls. "I'll stay home from church with your mother."

"Since your papa's away, I'll be taking you to church," announced Uncle Ralph, smiling at the children.

The Humphrey family went to the Methodist Church, a three-minute walk from their house. When Uncle Ralph and the children arrived at the church, an usher led them down the centre aisle to their family pew. It was the same one each week, third row from the front, on the right.

The service was long. As soon as it ended, Doug jumped up and looked around for his friend Bert. A raised hand waving a sock full of marbles caught Doug's eye. Doug, who had stuffed marbles into his pants pocket before leaving home, nodded at Bert with a big grin. Both boys ran out the side door of the church to play.

Ruth waited patiently outside while Uncle Ralph talked with his friends. As he chatted, Uncle Ralph spied Dr. Wetmore in his horse and carriage, driving out of the Humphrey's yard.

"Hmmm... it looks like Dr. Wetmore's already made one house call this morning," Uncle Ralph smiled with relief. "Come along, children. We best be getting home!"

Doug quickly put the marbles back in his pocket.

"Race you home, Ruth!" Doug yelled. "Last one to the door is a rotten egg!"

Doug reached the back door first.

From the gate, Ruth shouted, "That's not fair! You had a head start!"

Inside the house, Doug noticed an unusual quietness. As Ruth joined Doug in the kitchen, they heard a soft mewing sound coming from upstairs.

"What was that noise?" Ruth wondered aloud.

Doug shrugged, "Maybe a kitten?"

Aunt Bessie appeared on the stairs and cheerfully motioned to them.

"MY DEARS, YOU HAVE A NEW BABY BROTHER!"

"OH AUNT BESSIE!" cried Ruth, running up the stairs. "Can we see him?"

"Yes, but come quietly. Your mother is sleeping."

Ruth and Doug tiptoed as they followed Aunt Bessie down the hall to the bedroom door. Inside the bedroom, beside Mama's bed, the children saw a cradle. The new baby had arrived!

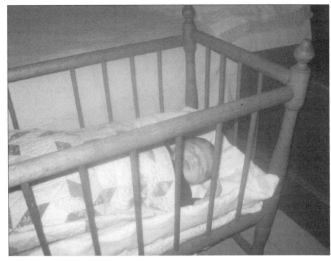
"I love you baby brother," Ruth whispered.

"HE'S SO TINY!" Ruth exclaimed.

Mama opened her eyes and spread her arms wide. The children promptly ran over and hugged her.

"What's his name?" Ruth asked, in awe.

"John Thomas Peters Humphrey," Mama said proudly.

Peeking into the cradle, Doug slid his arm between the rails and gently touched the top of his baby brother's head. Aunt Bessie looked on, thinking about the new baby she too would have in a few months.

"If it's a boy," she reflected, "I hope to name him Ralph."

Aunt Bessie smiled, thinking that he would make a good playmate someday for baby Johnny.

Ruth reached over and patted his soft hand. "I love you, baby brother," she whispered. Wondering aloud she asked, "Mama, what about Papa? We have to let him know about the baby!"

Aunt Bessie interjected, "I'll ask Uncle Ralph to send a telegram to your papa right away."

Just then Uncle Ralph peeked into the room.

"Congratulations, Nellie!" Uncle Ralph said, with a twinkle in his eye. "I saw Doc's carriage leaving your yard after church was over. I knew then the baby must have arrived safe and sound!"

Uncle Ralph assured Mama he would go immediately to the telegraph office so Papa would know about the new baby.

When in Montreal, Papa stayed at the Windsor Hotel.

In Montreal, Papa was leaning out the window of his hotel room, listening to the church bells. He was thinking about the two weeks of treatments the specialist had ordered. Hearing a knock at his door, Papa went and opened it. A hotel clerk handed him a telegram. Papa raised his eyebrows as he read it. A broad smile spread across his face.

WESTERN UNION TELEGRAM

RECEIVED AT ___ 1:25 P.M.   DATED___ APRIL 30, 1905

TO___ MR. FRANK HUMPHREY
      WINDSOR HOTEL
      MONTREAL, QUEBEC

Your home has been blessed this morning with another son.

"Thank you kindly, sir," Papa nodded. As the clerk hurried down the hallway, Papa called out, "It's a boy!"

"Now if I leave my hotel room within the hour, I can catch the three o'clock train to Saint John," Papa calculated. "I can't stay for treatments now. I have to see the baby!"

Ruth and Doug waited excitedly for Papa's train to arrive.

Papa sent Mama a telegram, letting her know he would be home the next day on the 4:20 train.

The whistle blew as the train approached Hampton Station. Ruth and Doug waited excitedly on the station platform. Papa was the first passenger off the train.

"PAPA!" screamed Ruth and Doug.

Papa stretched out his arms and gave them a big hug. Ruth took Papa by the hand.

"We have a new baby!" she exclaimed.

As Ruth skipped along beside him, Papa breathed excitedly, "I can hardly wait to see him!"

"I'm glad you're home," said Doug, as he reached out to help Papa carry his suitcase.

Papa grinned as he walked into the kitchen and saw Mama rocking the new baby.

"Love you, Nellie," he said softly, giving Mama a light kiss on the cheek.

Papa knelt down and gazed proudly at the baby.

"Hello, my dear son," he whispered. Stroking his soft fuzzy head, Papa added, "Oh Johnny, I love you very much."

Chapter 3

Where is Papa?

Large family gatherings were an important part of summer fun.

Johnny was a happy baby and well-loved by his family. Mama, however, had many sleepless nights as baby Johnny woke often wanting to be fed. Mama was so tired from being up during the night with Johnny that some mornings she found it hard to get out of bed. But she needed to prepare Papa's breakfast before he left for work on the early-morning train, and to see Ruth off to school.

One Saturday morning when Mama was getting ready to give Johnny a bath, Ruth asked, "Why does Johnny cry so much?"

"All babies cry," Mama explained. "It's their way of communicating."

"What do you mean?" Doug asked.

"How else can Johnny let us know he's hungry, or tired, or wants our attention?"

Ruth and Doug nodded in understanding. But they liked it better when Johnny smiled at them.

"There will be lots of time
to go boating," Papa said.

Mama was relieved to see Papa feeling better. Once again he was busy with the family shoe business and also with the local school board. As secretary of the board, Papa attended a lot of meetings because they were trying to build a new school in Hampton.

One Sunday after church, Papa announced, "Starting tomorrow I'll be on vacation."

"Yippee!" cried Ruth and Doug, giving Papa a hug.

"Will we go on lots of picnics?" Ruth asked.

"We already have our annual family picnic planned for next Sunday after church," Mama smiled.

Nodding at Doug, Papa said, "You and I'll take a few days and go trout fishing at my camp."

Doug was thrilled to hear that Papa would take him fishing at Lake Utopia.

"And there'll be lots of time for us all to go boating," Papa added.

Mama and the children enjoyed every day of Papa's vacation. All too soon summer holidays were over. Papa was back at work and the older children were in school.

At the end of the day, Johnny was all smiles when Papa arrived home from Saint John, ready for special Papa time. Their favourite game was when Papa bounced Johnny on his knee and sang, *"Oh, Johnny's horse is the fastest horse, the fastest horse you ever did see..."*

Papa was President of the Hampton Curling Club. In the early 1900s, young people curled outdoors on Ossekeag Creek.

During the winter, Papa curled. In January, he played only a few games before he felt too weak to throw the curling stone. Papa's illness had returned. For several months he struggled to get better. But sadly, Papa was critically ill. On a Monday morning in June, Papa passed away. He was only thirty-three years old.

SUSSEX, KINGS COUNTY, N.B. **THE KINGS COUNTY RECORD** JUNE 6, 1906 Price Two Cents

The Shiretown
[Hampton Station]

The death of Frank Monmouth Humphrey occurred at his home here, at 7:30 o'clock yesterday morning. The deceased had been in ill health for the past two years and during this time made several visits to Montreal where he underwent treatment... Although the best of medical skill was employed, nothing could be done but prolong his life for a brief period. The deceased was a member of the firm of JM Humphrey & Son of Saint John and had been a resident of Hampton all his life. He was a past master of the Corinthian Lodge #13, secretary of the local board of school trustees and president of Hampton Curling Club.

The community sustains a distinct loss in the removal of so exemplary a citizen. Funeral service will be held on Thursday afternoon from the home at 2:30. The family has the tenderest sympathy of the whole community in this their sad bereavement.

Throughout Papa's illness Mama had been so strong. But that morning as Papa drew his last breath, Mama cried.

"Oh my dear, I love you so very much," she sobbed. "I'll miss you terribly, Frank."

From the next room, Mama heard thirteen-month-old Johnny begin to cry. Slowly walking to his room, she picked Johnny up and cuddled him.

Mama tearfully told Ruth and then Doug that Papa had gone to heaven to be with God. As she gathered all three children around her, they shared in their sadness together.

The next day, when Mama read Papa's death notice in the newspaper, her eyes once more filled with tears.

Johnny's baby chant, "da-da-da", caused Mama to glance up from the newspaper. She noticed Johnny had a puzzled expression on his face as if he were looking for something. Mama watched as he pointed to Papa's rocking chair. She knew he was wondering where Papa was. Mama opened her arms and Johnny toddled over to her. She hugged him close.

"Johnny, I promise to tell you lots of stories about your father. Then when you're older you'll know how much he loved you."

Johnny pointed to Papa's
empty rocking chair.

Chapter 4

Toddler on the Tracks

Sixteen-month-old Johnny loved watching the trains go by in front of his house. He squealed with delight when the engineer blew the whistle.

"Too–tooo!" he'd exclaim.

One morning when Mama and Ruth were in the kitchen making red currant jelly, Johnny toddled outside. Neither one of them noticed that Johnny had stopped playing with his wooden blocks.

"Mama! The train! I hear it!" Ruth shouted.

"Oh my goodness," cried Mama, as she glanced toward the empty corner of the kitchen where Johnny had been playing. "Where is he now?!"

Mama and Ruth raced outside to search for Johnny.

Scanning the yard and railway tracks for any sign of him, Mama gasped, "For heaven's sakes!"

There was Johnny, toddling between the rails! Mama dashed toward him as fast as she could.

Following behind her, Ruth yelled, "MAMA! THE TRAIN! I HEAR IT!"

As she reached Johnny, Mama quickly scooped him up into her arms. The whistle blared. Mama glanced down the tracks and saw the train chugging toward them.

With Johnny clutched in one arm, Mama rushed back to Ruth and grabbed her hand. As they leapt off the tracks, Mama squeezed Johnny tightly to her.

"JOHNNY! NO! NO! NEVER GO ON THE RAILWAY TRACKS!"

When they returned to the kitchen, Mama was still shaking with fright.

"I'll have to keep a closer eye on you, my little adventurous son!" Mama determined.

Chapter 5

Wait for Me!

"Shoo! Shoo!" three-year-old Johnny called out, flapping his arms as he chased the crows that were eating the seeds in Mama's garden.

During his first three years, Johnny enjoyed playing in his yard, often with his cousin Ralph, who was the same age and lived three houses away.

Now four years old, Johnny looked forward to ten-year-old Ruth and nine-year-old Doug coming home from school. He would often sit on the back steps and wait for them. Sometimes Ruth and Doug played with Johnny. Other times they went off to play with their friends. Johnny hated being left behind.

When he felt really sad and left out, Johnny would wander down to the creek and launch his toy sailboat in the shallow water. While holding onto the string that was attached to his sailboat, Johnny watched the ducks. He also kept an eye on the

great blue heron standing at the edge of the water, waiting to catch fish with its long thin beak. The herons didn't seem to mind Johnny's sailboat bobbing along near them.

"I don't care if nobody plays with me," Johnny convinced himself, as he sat at the edge of the creek. "I'll have fun by myself!"

Johnny launched his toy sailboat in Ossekeag Creek.

Johnny's Cousin Jimmy, on Ossekeag Creek.

With the approach of winter, the children looked forward to sliding on the hill behind their house. One Saturday morning, Ruth ran upstairs to Doug's room.

"Doug, do you want to go sliding?"

Doug glanced out his back bedroom window and saw several children sliding down the hill. A new blanket of snow had fallen during the night, making the hill especially inviting.

"We've got the best sliding hill in Hampton Station!" Doug declared, racing down the stairs ahead of Ruth.

Johnny heard his sister and brother getting ready to go outside. He ran to the back porch where they were putting on their overshoes.

"Don't forget me, Rufus," said Johnny. "I want to slide too."

Ruth smiled at Johnny's nickname for her. Then she thought about what a handful he could be to look after.

"Pl-ea-se, Rufus!" Johnny pleaded.

Ruth recalled the time Papa had taken Doug to his fishing camp and hadn't taken her. She remembered how left out she had felt.

Reluctantly, Ruth agreed, "Yes, you can come, Johnny."

Mama came into the room, relieved that she would have time to finish her baking without interruption.

"I'll help you put on your woolen trousers, Johnny," Mama offered.

"This is the bestest," Johnny shouted.

As soon as he was dressed, Johnny burst out the door, followed by Ruth. They ran to catch up with Doug who was just bringing his toboggan to the top of the hill for another slide down.

"Come on, Johnny," exclaimed Doug, patting his toboggan. "Come sit right here."

Johnny was happy, wedged between his brother and sister. As they sped down the hill, Johnny grinned from ear to ear.

"This is the bestest!" Johnny shouted.

On another fast run, Johnny tumbled sideways and fell face-first into the snow.

"I want Mama!" Johnny cried, his face covered in snow.

"Don't be such a crybaby," Doug said, annoyed at his brother for making such a fuss.

"I'll wipe the snow off you," Ruth said, soothingly.

"MAMA!" Johnny cried louder, refusing to let anyone else comfort him.

Ruth sighed as she took her little brother back to the house. Hearing Johnny's insistent cry, Mama met them at the back door.

"I'll look after him," Mama assured Ruth. "You go back and play."

When Ruth and Doug finished sliding, they returned to the house, happy and hungry.

"M-m-m," Doug said, as he opened the back door. "I smell molasses cookies."

Johnny was curled up in the rocking chair beside the wood stove, munching on his second cookie. When he saw his brother and sister, Johnny hopped out of the rocking chair and grabbed two cookies.

"Cookie for you, Dougie; cookie for you, Rufus," Johnny called out, as he gave them each one.

In the spring, after the ice went out of the river, the neighbourhood boys began to talk about fishing.

When Doug arrived home from school one Friday afternoon, Mama reminded him, "If you plan to go fishing in the morning, you'll need to clean the ponies' stalls after supper."

"Sure, Mama."

Doug was so anxious to go fishing with his friends that he would have agreed to almost anything Mama wanted him to do.

Helping Mama set the table for supper, Johnny overheard the conversation.

"I want to go fishing!" Johnny exclaimed.

"You're too young to go," Doug answered.

"No, I'm not! I'll be five years old in eight more days and I know how to fish."

"But I'm going over to the river. You'll get too tired, and I'll have to stop and wait for you."

"No I won't. I promise!"

"Sorry, Johnny," Doug said firmly. "No tag-a-longs allowed."

"Doug," Mama whispered, "why don't you let Johnny go with you and see how he makes out?"

"No, Mama. He's too much trouble!"

The wharf in Hampton Village where boys went fishing.

39

Grandpa, who had been sitting in his rocking chair smoking his pipe, interrupted. "Doug, you take Johnny with you tomorrow or you'll stay home and help me split wood."

Doug frowned and turned his back on Grandpa. He had no choice. He would have to take Johnny with him.

Prancing around the kitchen, Johnny chanted, "I'm going fishing with Dougie! Lucky me!"

"You better go dig worms," Doug retorted, "enough for both of us."

Johnny stuck his tongue out at Doug and grinned as he ran off to get a shovel and start digging.

The next morning, Johnny woke at dawn. He tiptoed into Doug's bedroom.

Johnny gently lifted Doug's eyelid and whispered loudly, "Are you awake, Dougie?"

Doug batted him with his arm and rolled over.

"It's time to go fishing!" Johnny protested.

Doug opened his eyes and peered at his little brother. Johnny was all dressed and ready to go. Shaking himself awake, Doug changed into his clothes and went down to the kitchen. Mama had left the pot of oatmeal porridge on the back of the wood stove. Doug was stirring the porridge when Johnny ran into the kitchen.

"Doug, I want to get some apples to take with us but I can't open the cellar door. It's too heavy."

Following Johnny into the front hallway, Doug whispered in his ear, "Weakling!"

Grinning, Doug flexed his muscles and lifted the trap door as if it were as light as a feather.

"Jeepers," Johnny said, "why can't I do that?"

Johnny climbed down the ladder to the cellar. It was very dark but he used his nose to follow the wonderful smell coming from the apple barrels. Johnny chose two large Gravenstein apples and climbed back up the ladder.

After breakfast Doug made jam sandwiches. Then Johnny packed the sandwiches and apples in a metal pail. Grabbing their fishing gear, Doug walked and Johnny skipped along the road to the Kennebecasis River.

"Hurry up, Slowpoke," Doug called over his shoulder to Johnny, who had stopped to examine a large garter snake. "Bert's going to be there already," he shouted, hurrying ahead down the road.

"Hey, wait!" Johnny cried out, starting to run.

Doug reluctantly slowed down, giving Johnny a chance to catch up. By the time they arrived at the wharf, Bert and several other boys were already there, fishing.

"The only thing nibbling is some tiny perch," Bert lamented.

Doug and Johnny had no better luck than the others. At noontime, the boys decided to stop for lunch.

Munching on his sandwich, Johnny asked Doug, "Why is the river called the Kennebecasis?"

Bert piped up, "I know. My teacher told me. *Kennebec* means 'snake' and *sis* means 'little'."

Kennebec and *sis* are *Mi'kmaq* words. The *Mi'kmaq* are First Nations people who live on Canada's East Coast and in North-eastern Maine, USA.

"Little snake?" Johnny asked.

"The whole river twists and turns," Doug added, "like a snake."

"Like the snake I saw this morning?" asked Johnny.

"I guess so," Doug nodded.

"HOLY COW!" Johnny exclaimed, imagining all the curving riverbanks he had yet to explore.

While the boys continued fishing, Johnny began to daydream about soaring like an eagle over 'little snake' river. Suddenly there was a jerk on the end of his fishing rod.

"Johnny," shouted Doug, "you've got a fish!"

Frantic splashing came from the surface of the water as Johnny tried to reel in his line. Several boys came running over.

"It's a fighter!" Arthur yelled.

The Kennebecasis River, which twists and turns like a snake.

"Doug, help me!" Johnny cried, as the fish fought hard to get off his hook.

"You hold on to the rod and I'll reel it in," Doug directed.

Together, Johnny and Doug were able to land the fish safely on the wharf.

"Holy mackerel!" said Bert, as the other boys looked on. "That's the largest smallmouth bass I've ever seen! It must be twenty inches [fifty centimeters]!"

"WOW!" Johnny shouted excitedly, as he ran off the wharf, carrying his fish in the empty lunch pail. "I'm taking this home to Mama for supper!"

"Johnny," Doug called after him, "I'm not going home yet."

"But Dougie, I want Mama to see my fish."

"She will."

"NOW, DOUGIE, PLEASE!"

"No, Johnny! Not now! We'll go home after the riverboat gets here."

Doug and the other boys continued fishing. Placing the pail with his prized fish beside him, Johnny sat on the far end of the wharf and sulked.

*Johnny's mind began wandering to a trip Mama and Aunt Bessie were planning. The family would take the early-morning train into the city and sail back home on the riverboat, called the **SS Hampton.***

Johnny's aunts, uncles and cousins would be going. Grandpa Peters would also travel with them.

Johnny was looking forward to the family trip.

"It'll be fun eating on the riverboat!" Johnny had said when Mama first told him.

"Such a waste of good money," Grandpa had muttered as he puffed on his pipe.

"Imagine paying 35 cents each for dinner on the Hampton! I hope I'm not expected to pay for the whole family!"

The *Steamship Hampton,* which carried passengers and freight up and down the Kennebecasis River.

As Johnny wondered about what meal they would be served, the riverboat rounded the bend. Doug and his friends quickly packed up their fishing gear and waited for it to dock.

"When the *Hampton* gets close," Doug thought to himself, "Captain Mabee will be looking for older boys to tie the ropes to the wharf." Doug smiled confidently, because there weren't many big boys around.

"I think I'll get a chance to tie a rope today," Doug announced.

When a crew member threw one of the ropes ashore, Doug proudly caught and tied it – his first time to help moor the riverboat.

Gazing admiringly at his older brother, Johnny whispered to himself, "When I'm bigger, it'll be my turn to catch the rope."

Doug and his friends played tag on the way home. They ran ahead of Johnny who walked behind, dragging his heels.

"Hey, what about your brother?" Bert asked, noticing how far back he was.

"He's going slow on purpose," Doug assured his friends.

When Johnny lagged farther behind, he called out, "Hey, wait for me!"

The older boys stopped to wait, but as soon as Johnny caught up, they started running and playing tag again.

"You, Meanies!" Johnny cried out.

"Hey, we're not being mean," Bert yelled back. "You're just slow."

"Wait up," Johnny yelled after them.

This time, the older boys ignored him. Johnny sat on the ground and pouted, then finally got up and continued home. Upon reaching the railway station, he ran the rest of the way. Bursting through the back door, Johnny proudly held out his pail in front of Mama.

"Look at my fish, Mama! Isn't it a beauty!"

Seeing how excited Johnny was, Mama promised to cook the fish right away. While Johnny watched, Mama started preparing supper.

Later, when Mama called everyone to come eat, Johnny was nowhere to be found. Ruth went upstairs to check.

Running back down to the kitchen, Ruth laughed, "Guess what, Mama! Johnny's lying on his bed, and he's sound asleep!"

Chapter 6

A Kite Saves the Day

Six-year-old John

It was April 30, 1911 – Johnny's sixth birthday. Johnny was excited about his birthday party which would start at two o'clock that afternoon. But he had a few worries.

"Will my friends have fun at my party?" Johnny wondered. "I hope Mama makes sure everyone finds a penny in their piece of birthday cake!"

Grandpa Peters, however, was Johnny's biggest worry. "I hope Grandpa doesn't spoil my party. I know he'll want my friends to listen to one of his stories."

How many times had Johnny heard the story of Grandpa's double first cousin, Sir Leonard Tilley!

Sir Leonard Tilley,
Father of Confederation.

"Now Ruth, Doug and Johnny..." Grandpa would often say, as he sat in the rocking chair beside the wood stove, smoking his pipe.

"Come over here and sit down while I tell you about Cousin Leonard's trip to a conference in Charlottetown, over in Prince Edward Island. It was in September, 1864, before the railroad was built on the Island..."

As he puffed perfect donut circles of smoke into the air to get their full attention, Grandpa insisted, "You must never forget Cousin Leonard because he was one of the Fathers of Confederation. Thanks to Cousin Leonard, that conference in Charlottetown led to Canada becoming a country... My father told me that Cousin Leonard was knighted Sir Leonard by Queen Victoria herself!"

Grandpa always finished the story by claiming, "Sir Leonard got his brains from the Peters side of the family, of course!"

To keep Grandpa happy, Johnny and the other grandchildren always listened to his stories as if they were hearing them for the first time.

Johnny hoped Grandpa would go over to the train station in the afternoon as he usually did, and talk to whoever happened to be around. Shortly before two o'clock, Johnny breathed a sigh of relief when he saw Grandpa walking across the street toward the station.

Soon after the party started, the children lined up to play Pin-the-Tail-on-the-Donkey. When it was Johnny's turn, Doug whirled him around three times. Blindfolded, Johnny staggered forward. The other children laughed as Johnny tried to attach the donkey's tail to the side of the piano. After everyone had a turn, Mama suggested they go outside and play.

As the children ran out the back door, Johnny shouted, "Let's play hide and seek!"

"I'll be 'it'," Doug called out. "Go hide, everybody. I'll count to twenty." The children scampered off; some went behind the shed and others ran to hide behind Grandpa's apple trees.

Train Station: Johnny and his family lived in the white house, center back.

While Grandpa walked back from the train station, he thought, "I'd better tell Johnny's friends a story. I don't want to disappoint those youngsters... I think I'll tell them about Sir Leonard."

On the front veranda, Grandpa spied one of Johnny's birthday gifts. It was a kite. With a grin on his face, Grandpa remembered the fun he'd had making and flying kites as a boy. Grandpa grabbed the kite and wandered into the backyard. He held the kite up until the wind caught it, then let out the string. Soon the kite was as high as the rooftops.

Johnny looked up from his hiding place and whispered, "My kite! Grandpa's flying my new kite!"

Opening up the back door, Mama looked at Johnny, who seemed to be lost in thought as he stared at his grandfather. Mama smiled at her father as he released more string, allowing the kite to fly higher.

"Johnny, it's time to blow out the candles on your cake," Mama called.

Grandpa remembered flying kites as a boy.

47

Peppermint sticks and lemon drops were favourite candies.

Full of excitement, the children cheered as they ran inside.

"There are surprises hidden in the cake... so be careful," Mama advised.

Young Ralph's fork clinked.

"I found a penny!" Ralph announced gleefully.

Before long, all the children had found a penny in their piece of cake.

"Yippee!" cried the children, knowing they'd be going to the General Store to buy some penny candy.

When it was time to go home, Johnny's friends thanked Mama for a wonderful party. Johnny smiled as he said good-bye to his friends.

"I'm so glad Grandpa was flying my kite," breathed Johnny. "He forgot to tell one of his long boring stories!"

When Mama tucked Johnny into bed that night, he said, "Mama, this has been the best birthday ever!"

"I'm glad, Johnny," answered Mama, giving him a big hug. "Now that you're six, you will soon be starting school."

"Mama," Johnny requested, "since I'm almost in school, I want to be called John."

"That's fine, John. I'll do my best to remember that."

John lay in bed thinking how happy he was to finally be six years old. He was looking forward to entering Grade 1 in August.

That night John dreamed he was soaring to school, hanging onto the end of a kite-string, with his older brother and sister breathlessly running behind.

Chapter 7

Playing with Fire

"Mama," six-year-old John cried out, "Uncle Leonard just got off the train. I think he has some presents for us!"

Boy in a playsuit, 1911.

In the early 1900s, the Eaton's Catalogue sold "Boys' Play Suits". There were playsuits for dressing up like a pirate, a cowboy, a doctor, and a First Nations' boy. The playsuit in the above photo was made by non-aboriginals and was a stereotype idea of what First Nations' boys wore.

Playsuits were often ordered from the catalogue [$1.25] and given as a gift.

It was a hot July day and Mama's brother, Leonard, was all smiles as he strolled toward the Humphrey house. Having shopped at Manchester's popular department store in Saint John, Uncle Leonard had bought three presents: an *Anne of Green Gables* book for Ruth, a fishing reel for Doug, and a playsuit for John.

"Wow! That's swell!" John exclaimed, admiring his present.

With help from Mama, John quickly tried it on.

"Thank you, Uncle Leonard," John grinned, giving his uncle a quick hug as he hurried outside where his friends were waiting for him.

When Cousin Ralph saw John's new playsuit, he ran over for a closer look.

"Where did you get this?" Ralph asked enviously, fingering the long shiny fringes on the sleeves.

"Uncle Leonard gave it to me," John replied proudly.

"You are so lucky, John!" Ralph exclaimed. "I wish I had one like yours."

John beamed. He loved his new playsuit!

As John glanced behind the shed, he spied his friend, Douglas (not to be confused with his brother Doug), taking matches out of his pocket.

John's big grin changed into a nervous smile.

"Let's light some!" Douglas suggested eagerly.

"Mama told me not to play with matches," said John.

John debated what to do. He thought, "I don't know what to say. I don't want to miss out on the fun, but...

Two of the Humphrey's ponies, before the fire.

It was four months ago when Mama talked to John about the dangers of playing with matches, right after their barn and carriage house had burned to the ground. It had been a spectacular, but frightening blaze. No one knew how the fire had started. At the time, Mama was terrified the fire would spread and that their house might burn as well.

The family was dreadfully upset because their horse, named Magna Carta, and seven ponies died in the fire. For several nights afterward, John cried over Ginger, his favourite pony.

maybe, if we're careful, it'll be alright."

Ralph and Douglas looked expectantly at John, waiting for his answer.

"As long as Mama doesn't find out," John bargained.

"She'll never know," Ralph and Douglas promised.

"Let's light the matches down by the creek," John suggested.

The boys raced down to Ossekeag Creek, away from John's house. At the edge of the creek, beside an abandoned house, was an old outhouse.

"Shall we try the outhouse?" Ralph asked. "No one will see us in there and we can throw the matches down the hole."

"Shall we try the outhouse?"

"Sure," the other two nodded.

After prying open the outhouse door, the three boys squeezed inside.

"I'll light the first one," Douglas offered.

Following a couple of failed tries, the match sparked and flamed.

"There it goes!" Ralph grinned, as Douglas dropped the match down the hole.

When it hit the water in the creek at the bottom of the hole, John squealed with delight, "Wow! Did you hear it sizzle?!"

The boys took turns lighting more, and before long they ran out of matches.

"I know where there are more matches," John said, excitedly. "I'll be right back."

John ran to his house and sneaked upstairs, unseen by Mama who was talking with Grandpa on the front veranda. In the bathroom there was a box of matches, which Mama kept there to light the oil lamp at night. John took some and put them in his pocket.

Ralph and Douglas thought it would be more fun if they had pieces of paper to burn as well. So while John was gone, the boys ripped out pages from an old Eaton's Catalogue they found on the floor of the outhouse. (The catalogue had been put there for use as toilet paper – one page at a time.) As John ran back to the outhouse, the shiny fringes on his playsuit flapped in the wind.

Pages from the Eaton's Catalogue, 1901.

The burning paper spiralled downward, missing the toilet hole.

"I want to light the match," John said, as he took one out of his pocket.

"Okay," Douglas agreed, crumpling a page of the catalogue. "I'll hold the paper."

Peering out around the outhouse door, Ralph said, "I'll keep a look-out."

Douglas held the crumpled paper over the flame until it caught fire.

"YIKES! IT'S HOT!" Douglas yelled, dropping the burning page.

The paper spiralled downward, missing the toilet hole and landing on top of the old catalogue. The boys watched in horror as the catalogue burst into flames.

"HOLY COW!" Ralph shrieked.

John quickly tried to stamp out the flames.

"HELP ME!" he shouted.

The boys all stamped their feet, doing their best to put out the fire. But flames licked up higher, climbing rapidly up the dry-wood wall.

"JOHN!" Douglas shouted as he pointed to the fringe on the left sleeve of John's playsuit, "YOU'RE ON FIRE!"

Ralph darted out the door, yelling, "LET'S GET OUT OF HERE!"

Back outside, the boys stared in shock as the flames engulfed John's left arm. John started to panic as he watched the flames eating through his playsuit and begin burning his skin. He screamed in pain.

"WE NEED HELP!" Ralph cried.

"RUN!" yelled Douglas.

Waving his arm in the air, John ran up the hill from the creek and into a near-by backyard, howling. Racing behind him, the boys were petrified to see the flames leaping higher.

Neighbours heard the uproar and hurried outside. To their horror, they saw a frantic young boy whirling inside a sheet of fire!

"GOOD LORD!" shouted Walter Conway, the baggage master from the railway station. Grabbing a piece of carpet, Walter ran to John and quickly wrapped him up, smothering the flames.

Aunt Bessie frantically cranked the handle of her telephone.

Startled to hear a heavy pounding on her back door, Mama hurried to open it.

"Nellie!" shrieked Pauline, Mama's next-door neighbour, "YOUR SON'S ON FIRE!"

"MERCIFUL HEAVENS!" Mama cried and ran for all she was worth to where John lay on the grass. Her heart pounded with fright as John writhed and howled in pain.

Ralph and Douglas ran home to hide. Ralph's mother, Aunt Bessie, saw young Ralph dashing upstairs to his bedroom, and stopped him.

"Ralph! You're as white as a ghost! What on earth is going on?"

"John's arm caught on fire!" Ralph blurted out. "Mr. Conway put the fire out but John's lying on the ground, screaming. Aunt Nellie's with him."

Aunt Bessie glanced out her back window, then ran and frantically cranked the handle of her telephone.

"MILLIE," Bessie cried hysterically, to the operator who connected the circuits. "RING 1-2, FOR DR. WETMORE! EMERGENCY! YOUNG JOHN HUMPHREY'S BEEN BURNED!"

The telephones were party lines. Five homes on the same line could listen in on one another's conversations. In no time at all, operator Millie called Bessie back. The neighbours knew that two short rings meant the call was for Ralph and Bessie March.

Several people picked up their phones and heard Millie say, "The good doctor is on

Operator Millie quickly connected the circuits.

53

his way, Bessie. I hope young John's not too badly burned."

Within a very short time, everyone in Hampton Station knew that John Humphrey had caught on fire.

As she sat on the grass beside John, Mama sobbed quietly and tried to comfort him.

Two nurses, who were staying at the nearby Wayside Inn, had heard the commotion. They ran over to attend to John. After glancing down at his charred playsuit, they exchanged worried looks.

"I hope the doctor comes soon," the nurse with the graying hair whispered.

"Me too!" murmured the younger nurse. "His pulse is very rapid. This is serious!"

Ten minutes later, Dr. Wetmore and Dr. Smith arrived. After a quick check of John's condition, the doctors had him carried back to his house and upstairs to his bedroom. With John settled in his bed, the doctors carefully peeled back his clothes and examined John's arm.

"This is a very bad burn, Mrs. Humphrey," Dr. Smith commented.

While Mama tried to comfort John, Dr. Smith gently washed his left arm. Dr. Wetmore started peeling off burnt skin. Because the nerve endings in his arm were badly damaged, John couldn't feel the burnt skin being removed.

Grandpa was pacing back and forth in the kitchen when Ruth and Doug arrived home from visiting at a friend's house. Glancing at Grandpa's troubled face, Ruth knew that something was wrong. After Grandpa told them the awful news, Ruth and Doug rushed to the bottom of the stairs.

Grandpa warned harshly, "You are not to go upstairs until the doctors have gone."

It was nearly an hour later when the doctors finished cleaning the wound and wrapping his arm in gauze.

"John's in shock," Dr. Wetmore explained to Mama. "Keep him warm for now, and drinking fluids. I'll return tomorrow to change the gauze."

As soon as the doctors left, Ruth and Doug raced upstairs and peeked into John's bedroom.

"OH, NO!" Ruth gasped as she gazed at John shifting restlessly on the bed.

"Is he going to be okay?" Doug asked fearfully.

Mama was sitting on the side of John's bed and motioned for them to leave. She was humming softly, hoping that John would fall asleep. As Ruth and Doug closed the door, they heard John utter a soft moan.

The next day, John was very uncomfortable and still suffering from shock. His arm hurt and it was difficult for him to move. Mama kept encouraging him to eat and drink.

While Mama was taking molasses cookies (John's favourite) out of the oven, she heard a knock at the back door. It was young Ralph.

"You want to see John?" Mama asked, quietly.

Without looking up, Ralph nodded his head.

"He's sleeping, but you can go upstairs and see him."

Sitting quietly beside John's bed, Ralph held John's good right hand. He was horrified to see John's left arm wrapped in white gauze from his shoulder to his wrist.

John opened his eyes briefly and whispered, "Ralph."

Tears ran down Ralph's face as he replied, "I'm sorry, John! I didn't know this would happen!"

John squeezed Ralph's hand to let him know he understood. He closed his eyes again and drifted back to sleep.

Over the next several days, Ralph returned to silently hold John's hand for hours at a time.

This act of kindness would be remembered and treasured by John for the rest of his life.

Chapter 8

Mama's Worst Fear

Saint John General Public Hospital, where John had several surgeries.

The doctors did their best to save John's arm. Over the next few weeks, Dr. Wetmore came daily to change the gauze and clean his wound. As the nerve endings in John's arm started to heal, the pain became excruciating. It was so painful that there was nothing else John could do but scream.

Several times during the fall and winter, John went to the Saint John General Public Hospital for surgery. Dr. White grafted skin, donated by Mama's friends, Fannie and Minnie, onto John's arm.

Every time Mama earnestly prayed, "Please God, help John's arm heal."

But after each surgery, John's body rejected the newly-grafted skin. Because his wound was red and continually oozing liquid, it was very painful to touch. John hated having the dressings changed because the gauze stuck to the oozing spots and dried like glue. When the dressings were changed, the wound would re-open and the pain was unbearable.

John pleaded with the nurses, "Take the gauze off slowly, please!"

"No, John," one nurse replied, matter-of-factly, "quicker is better."

John howled, kicked and screamed as they stripped off the gauze, washed the wound and rewrapped his raw red arm.

Eventually the wound healed well enough for John to go home.

One morning, when Ruth and Doug were at school and Grandpa was at the railway station, John confided in his mother.

"Mama, I hate the... the clora... you know, what the doctors put me to sleep with, before my operations."

Mama nodded, "Chloroform?"

"YES, I'M...I'M AFRAID...I WON'T WAKE UP AGAIN!"

Before each surgery, John put up such a fight in the operating room that the medical team strapped his good arm to the operating table, to hold him down. What the doctors and nurses didn't realize was that John was struggling because he was scared he would die.

Mama held John close, being careful not to touch his painful left arm.

"You don't need to worry, John. God will take care of you. And Dr. White will make sure you wake up after every surgery."

In the operating room, John put up a fight.

John smiled, somewhat relieved. But whenever another surgery was scheduled, John began to worry all over again.

In addition to his fears about dying, John dreadfully missed doing fun things with his friends.

One cold, snowy afternoon, John stood at his bedroom window and enviously watched some children sliding down the hill.

John's friends, Ralph and Douglas, looked up at the

From his bedroom window, John enviously watched the children sliding.

window and waved to him. As John waved back, there was a lump in his throat. He tried his hardest to hold back the tears. John felt so sad to be cut off from his friends like this!

That night John slowly climbed into bed, carefully protecting his left arm as he got settled. John thought of all the painful operations he'd undergone, which hadn't helped him. And every night in his bedtime prayers, he asked God to make his arm better. That hadn't worked either. John felt very discouraged.

When Mama arrived to tuck John into bed and to hear him say his prayers, John asked her, "Why is it taking so long for my arm to heal? It's not fair! I have nobody to play with! I have to stay inside and all my friends are playing outdoors!" John started to weep. "AND THEY'RE ALL IN GRADE 1 WITHOUT ME!"

"I know this year has been very difficult for you John, but we won't give up," Mama tried to reassure him.

Pupils at Hampton Consolidated, 1911.

"Remember, I love you very much and God loves you."

"Then why doesn't God make my arm better?"

"I don't know, John. But we can't give up hope. Sometimes we don't understand God's plan for us."

As John wiped away another tear, Mama started singing two of John's favourite church songs – *Jesus Loves Me* and *Onward Christian Soldiers.*

When Mama returned to the empty kitchen, she whispered tearfully, "How I wish the doctors could save my son's arm!" With all her heart she prayed, "Please God, help us!" Mama held onto the sink as she doubled over, sobbing quietly, "Papa, where are you now when I need you? Please ask God to send an angel to help us!"

On April 30, 1912, Uncle Leonard arrived on the train from Saint John for John's 7th birthday. When the family finished celebrating John's special day with cake and presents, Uncle Leonard took Mama aside.

"I'd like to take John to Montreal," Uncle Leonard suggested, "to see if there's a doctor there who can save his arm. The doctors in Saint John have tried for nine months, Nellie, and John's arm is still not better!"

Mama agreed. "If there is a better chance for success, then he should go. Thank you, Leonard."

Two weeks later, John and Uncle Leonard went to Montreal. Mama prepared John for travelling by lightly wrapping his arm in a cotton cloth and putting a sling over his opposite shoulder. The sling would help support his raw, almost lifeless, arm.

Union Station: train station in Saint John, N.B. (location of present-day Harbour Station)

59

"All aboard!" the conductor shouted.

"All aboard!" the conductor shouted.

Mama, Ruth and Doug gave John a hug, mindful of his left arm, before he and Uncle Leonard climbed on board.

After everyone was on the train, the conductor signaled with an up-and-down hand motion. The engineer gave two long blasts with the whistle; the train then slowly left Hampton Station.

John was excited about the trip, but nervous about going to see another doctor. He hated having anyone touch, or worse still, operate on his arm. But as the train gained speed, John's attention was focused on the adventure – an overnight train ride to the big city of Montreal!

"Will we really sleep on the train?" John quizzed Uncle Leonard. "Will we be in Montreal tomorrow? How many whistle posts are there between Saint John and Montreal?"

"Well, there has to be a whistle post placed in advance of every road that crosses the railway tracks…" Uncle Leonard explained.

"I know," John interjected. "The posts tell the engineers when to blow the train's whistle. Then people don't cross the tracks and get hurt!"

Uncle Leonard chuckled, "Yes. And there must be quite a few country roads crossing the tracks, between here and Montreal!"

"Uncle Ralph told me that each engineer has his own special way of blowing the whistle," John rattled on, excitedly. "Is that true, Uncle Leonard? Have you ever been on the train to Montreal before? Mama told me that Papa took the same train when he went to Montreal!" John added proudly.

Uncle Leonard listened to John and tried to answer his many questions. Eventually John fell asleep, and soon after Uncle Leonard started snoring.

Whistle post, Hampton, N.B.

John woke up to the sound of the train's whistle. In a booming voice, the conductor called out,

"NEXT STOP – WINDSOR STATION – MONTREAL – NEXT STOP!"

Windsor Train Station, across the street from the Windsor Hotel, Montreal.

The train pulled up inside the huge Windsor Station. When John and Uncle Leonard got off the train, they walked out to the street. John's eyes grew wide in amazement.

"This is big! Look at all the fancy carriages, Uncle Leonard! And the streetcars!"

"That's where we'll be staying," Uncle Leonard pointed across the street, "the Windsor Hotel."

"Is that where Papa stayed?" John asked.

"Yes, that's where your father stayed, eight years ago," Uncle Leonard replied.

Main corridor of the Windsor Hotel, 1916.

John fingered the pocket watch that Dr. White had given him.

The hotel entrance was grand. John had never seen anything so luxurious in all his life! A bellhop, dressed in a well-pressed uniform, with a little round cap on his head, picked up their luggage and carried it to the elevator door.

"These gentlemen have a room on the sixth floor," the bellhop informed the elevator operator.

When they reached the top floor, the operator opened the double set of elevator doors and sang out, "Sixth floor! Watch your step, please."

Entering their room, Uncle Leonard remarked grandly. "John, come look out the window."

John scurried over and peered out cautiously.

"We're up so high!" John said in amazement. "Look at the people. They look as small as my toy soldiers!"

Watching a streetcar go by, John remembered his appointment at the hospital the next morning.

"Uncle Leonard, tomorrow when we go on the streetcar, I'm scared someone will bump my arm."

"Don't worry about that, John," Uncle Leonard assured him. "We'll take a carriage in the morning."

That evening when John lay down on the bed, his head was spinning.

"I hope the doctors in Montreal are as nice as Dr. White," John worried, as he fingered the pocket watch that his surgeon in Saint John had given him. "I'm so glad Dr. White gave me this – my very first watch!"

As he placed his watch on the bedside table, John tried imagining what the Montreal doctors might say to him.

"John Humphrey, we're the big-city doctors and we know everything. Your arm will be better before you know it!"

John fell asleep, praying that everything would be alright.

Royal Victoria Hospital, Montreal, early 1900s.

In the morning, John and Uncle Leonard went by horse and carriage to the Royal Victoria Hospital. As they stepped onto the street, John stopped and stared at the enormous building.

"I don't want to go in there!"

"It's alright, John," Uncle Leonard assured him, as he took John by the hand. "I'll be with you the whole time. I won't leave you."

The nurse was kind to John while they waited for the doctor to arrive. Her friendly manner helped John feel more comfortable.

After examining John's arm, the doctor said, "Knowing how far you have travelled for this appointment, I'll call in another doctor."

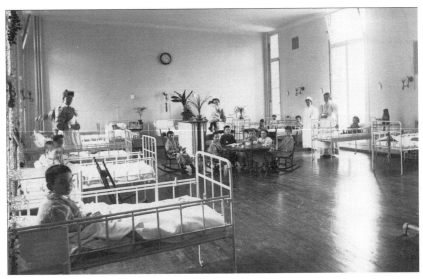

Royal Victoria Hospital, children's ward.

Turning to Uncle Leonard, he spoke reassuringly, "We'll get a second opinion and then we'll be sure to do what's best for this boy."

Both doctors examined John's arm very carefully, asking questions about previous treatments he had received in Saint John. While the nurse stayed with John, the two doctors asked Uncle Leonard to step outside the room with them. They spoke quietly so John couldn't hear them. Uncle Leonard returned to John, trying to hide his disappointment.

"We're all done," said Uncle Leonard. "Let's go back to the hotel. You can order a nice dessert, and we'll have it delivered to our room."

John was elated. "You mean, I don't have to stay for an operation?"

"That's right," Uncle Leonard managed to say, as he fought back tears of frustration.

Uncle Leonard looked away for a few seconds so John couldn't see his face. He felt like he had failed, by taking John on a useless trip. But he knew that at least he had tried. There was nothing more that could be done for John.

Intercolonial Railway, Parlour Car.

"I'll not say anything to John, now," Uncle Leonard decided. "I must let him enjoy the trip home... I'll break the news to Nellie and she can tell John herself."

The following day, John and Uncle Leonard took the train home. It was a long ride but John enjoyed exploring the train cars. His favourite was the parlour car.

John slept all night, lulled to sleep by the rhythm of the wheels and the happy thought that he didn't have to stay in Montreal for an operation.

When they arrived in Saint John at noon, John and Uncle Leonard changed trains. The connecting train travelled the tracks along the Kennebecasis River Valley. This countryside was very familiar to John. He eagerly began counting the whistle posts – just five more to go!

"There's Lakeside Station," John called out to Uncle Leonard, as he pressed his nose against the train window. "Next stop is Hampton Station! I bet Mama will be waiting for me!"

As the train slowed down to a stop, John beamed when he caught sight of Mama, Ruth and Doug, standing on the station platform. Mama gave him an excited kiss on the cheek. Ruth and Doug were happy to see John, too, and each gave him a gentle hug. John had lots of stories to tell – about room service, bellhops, and the train ride.

After supper, the children ran upstairs to look through John's suitcase and see the little gifts that Uncle Leonard had bought for them. Now that they were alone in the kitchen, Uncle Leonard had a chance to speak with Mama.

"I'm sorry, Nellie," Uncle Leonard said, wiping a tear that welled in his eye, his voice trembling. "The doctors said there was nothing they could do for John. They examined him carefully… They said his arm will never heal!"

Mama's face turned pale. She was devastated to learn this news, but tried to keep herself from crying. She had put so much hope and faith for John's recovery into their trip to see the big-city doctors. She had felt sure that this would be the answer to her prayers.

"MY WORST FEAR COME TRUE!" Mama started to cry. "HOW CAN I TELL JOHN?"

Uncle Leonard put a comforting arm around Mama. "It'll be alright, somehow, Nellie. God will provide an answer."

Mama stood in silence, trying to gather her thoughts. "What should I do?" she wondered.

"I must call Dr. Wetmore," Mama decided. "We need to know if there is another option. John can't go through life like this." Mama's voice started to crack under the strain. "The way he is now, he can't play, or go to school, or do any of the things that other children do!"

Chapter 9

Gone!

D r. Wetmore sat in the Humphrey's front parlour, prepared to talk with John. He wasn't looking forward to this conversation. With a heavy heart, Mama sat on the sofa beside her son. Taking a deep breath, Dr. Wetmore began.

"John, it's been nearly a year since your accident and your arm has not healed. It was a severe burn, and unfortunately the wound is large, stretching all the way up to your shoulder. I'm afraid it will never heal well enough for you to use. It will always be raw, sore, and subject to infections." Observing John's confused look, Dr. Wetmore continued, cautiously. "You know, John, these infections could attack other parts of your body and pose a great danger to you."

The grandfather clock chimed the hour.

John stared at the grandfather clock in the front hallway and said nothing. He was afraid of what Dr. Wetmore might say next.

"Tomorrow, your mother will take you on the early morning train into Saint John, to the hospital."

"NO! NOT ANOTHER OPERATION!" John shouted, starting to panic.

"This will be your last operation," Dr. Wetmore assured him. "You know Dr. White, of course."

John slipped his hand into the right pocket of his pants and clutched the watch Dr. White had given him.

"Dr. White will amputate your arm," Dr. Wetmore said, as the grandfather clock chimed the hour.

"What does am-pu-tate mean?" John asked, glancing worriedly at his mother.

Seeing how upset Mama looked, he thought, "It must be something bad!"

Doctor Wetmore hesitated. "Do you remember the older boy, named William, who was in the hospital the last time you were there for a skin graft?"

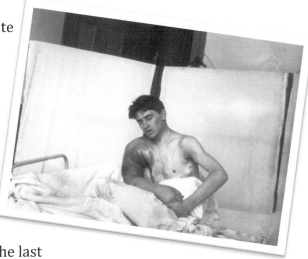

"Remember William? The doctor amputated his arm too."

John nodded his head.

"Dr. White amputated his right arm shortly after you left the hospital. William was suffering with a badly-infected arm, but now he is fine."

"But what does am-pu-tate **mean**?" John insisted.

Dr. Wetmore looked over at John's mother, who nodded for him to carry on.

"Dr. White will have to cut off your arm... right here, at the shoulder." As tears welled up in John's eyes, Dr. Wetmore continued, "Dr. White is an excellent surgeon. You will have the very best of care."

Cradling his left arm with his right hand, John tramped out of the room, yelling, "NO ONE'S GOING TO CUT OFF **MY** ARM!"

Mama and Dr. Wetmore could hear John stomping up the stairs, followed by a loud bang as he slammed his bedroom door. Mama's eyes filled with tears. She had known it would be difficult to tell John. But she was relieved that he finally knew what was ahead of him. Mama thanked Dr. Wetmore for his help and walked with him to the front door.

"Tomorrow will be a difficult day for you, Mrs. Humphrey." Placing his hand on top of Mama's, Dr. Wetmore added, "God be with you."

Mama could hear that John was still crying in his bedroom. She hurried upstairs.

"I don't want the doctor to cut off my arm!" John cried. "It'll hurt!"

"They'll give you some medicine so you won't feel any pain," Mama assured him.

"But what can I do with only one arm?" John asked fearfully. "What will my friends say?"

Mama sat down on the bed beside John and gave him a hug.

"Your true friends will always

"Will Uncle Leonard be driving his new Model T?"

be your good friends, no matter what."

John was somewhat comforted, thinking, "I've already learned to button my shirt with one hand. And I only needed one hand to beat Doug at crokinole...but, I don't want to lose my arm... not my whole arm!"

Continuing to hold John close, Mama said, "In the morning when we get to Saint John, Uncle Leonard will meet us at Union Station and take us to the hospital."

"Will Uncle Leonard be driving his new Model T?" John asked.

"Yes, my dear, and you can ride up front with him."

Knowing it was important for John to get his sleep, Mama suggested, "You snuggle down in bed and I'll read you a story."

As she read, John drifted off to sleep. Mama leaned over and kissed him.

"God bless you," she whispered.

The next day when John awoke from surgery, the first thing he saw was his mother's face. As she stood at his bedside in the children's ward, Mama smiled wearily.

"Mama, my arm," he whispered. "It feels like it's still there... but

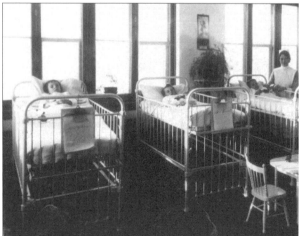

Children's Ward in a New Brunswick Hospital.

it's not heavy anymore!"

John used his right hand to reach over and touch his left shoulder. "It's - it's GONE!" he whimpered.

His mother nodded, fighting back tears.

That afternoon, Doctor White stopped by. He looked at John lying in the bed.

Noticing John's tear-stained face, Dr. White spoke quietly, "I'm very sorry, John."

Dr. White worried for John's future with only one arm. Yet, he reasoned, if anyone had a chance at making a great recovery and life for himself, it was John Humphrey.

"John, I saw you reading a children's book in my office."

"I've come to know you quite well over the last year, John. You have lots of spunk," Dr. White smiled. "Remember how you fought us every time on the operating table, determined not to give in to the chloroform? And I saw you reading a children's book in my office. You know how to read and you haven't even started school!" Dr. White admired.

"I also remember how quickly you learned to tell time, after I gave you a watch. You're a smart boy, John." Patting him kindly on his remaining arm, the doctor nodded, "I know you'll figure out a way to manage with one arm."

Each day Dr. White came to the children's ward to check on his young patient.

"Your arm is healing very quickly, John!" Dr. White smiled.

Ten days after the surgery when Dr. White made his rounds, he declared, "John, you can go home tomorrow."

John grinned, "Thank you, Dr. White. I hardly have any more pain!"

Dr. White turned to Mama who was sitting in a chair at the foot of John's bed.

"Mrs. Humphrey, I recommend you take John on a vacation, near the ocean. It's time this boy had some fun!"

Dr. White winked at John. "Good luck, young man!"

The next day, Mama arrived early at the hospital. She smiled when she saw John all dressed, with his packed suitcase at the foot of his bed.

"Uncle Leonard's outside," Mama said. "We'll take the 10:45 train and be in Hampton before your sister and brother get home for lunch."

Just minutes after John and Mama arrived home, Ruth and Doug burst through the back door.

"Glad you're home," Ruth smiled, giving John a hug.

"Welcome home, little brother," Doug said. "Let's eat. I'm hungry!"

They had barely finished their lunch when Cousin Ralph appeared at the back door. Ralph tried not to stare, but his eyes kept returning to the spot where John's arm used to be. John was embarrassed and didn't know what to say. Finally, Ralph spoke.

"Want to play a game of marbles before I go back to school?" he asked.

"You bet," John said with a big grin.

John ran upstairs and grabbed his sock full of marbles. Then the boys raced outside to their favourite spot behind the shed.

"There are only two weeks of school left," Ralph told John. "After that I can play with you every day."

The whole community heard about John's amputation and wanted to do nice things that would cheer him up. William Barnes, the young telegraph operator, offered to give John lessons on how to handle a sabre.

"It's good for you to be able to defend yourself," Mr. Barnes explained to John, when they arrived at his barn.

John was excited. He always wanted to be a soldier.

The next evening while Mama was carrying a straw basket of clean laundry past Doug's bedroom, she overheard a conversation.

"Have you ever held a sabre?" John asked Doug.

"No, have you?"

"Yes," John nodded.

"When?" questioned Doug.

"Yesterday, when you were at school," John grinned. "Mr. Barnes took me out to his barn. He let me hold his sabre. It's very heavy!"

"Mr. Barnes let me hold his sabre!" John grinned.

70

"Wow!" Doug said, enviously.

"Tomorrow, he's going to teach me how to thrust the sword, right into a bale of hay!"

Mama could hardly believe her ears. "This is my son who just had his arm amputated!"

She put down her laundry basket and rushed over to Barnes' Store, fuming.

With hands on her hips, Mama said firmly, "William, I don't want any more accidents. JOHN IS NOT TO USE A SABRE!"

William nodded, knowing full well what Mama meant. The sabre lessons ceased.

As soon as Ruth and Doug finished the school year, Mama took her three children to Red Head for a vacation. Red Head Beach was on the Bay of Fundy coast with a view of Saint John. Mama smiled as she watched the children playing in the sand which stretched between two rocky seaweed-covered points.

"Want to add a tower to your castle?" Doug asked John.

"Yes!" John smiled, picking up the metal pail with his remaining hand.

Doug added water to John's pail and helped him tip it upside down to make a tower. Ruth dug a moat around the castle.

By the time the second week of vacation had rolled around, John's shoulder had almost completely healed. Now he could splash around in the salt water.

Mama smiled as she watched the children play.

"Mama," John called out as he ran down the beach, jumping over seaweed and chasing gulls into the air, "I love it here!"

Mama waved back at John, happy to see him having so much fun. How fast he seemed to be adjusting to life with one arm.

Many years later, John would look back and remember the summer he'd spent in Red Head as one of the best summers of his life.

Chapter 10

School Days

Hampton Consolidated School, built in 1907.

The community was proud of Hampton Consolidated School, a large modern building located between Hampton Station and Hampton Village.

The school had opened in 1907, when John was two years old. John's father Frank had been secretary of the school board when the trustees had worked on the plans for the new school. At that time, John was only a baby.

During their planning meetings, the trustees discussed the school layout.

Hampton Consolidated School van.

"Of course, we'll have two entrances to the school," one of them said. "The boys will enter the building through one door and the girls will enter through the other."

"There will be indoor toilets in the basement," Frank reminded them, pointing to the paper design. "The plans show long enamel troughs the length of the room, with separate stalls. This will be costly but much improved over outhouses."

Before the new school opened, the trustees arranged for a school van to transport pupils who lived a long distance from the school. The large wooden box would seat about twenty children. The driver used his own team of horses to pull the van.

During the winter, the school provided a big box sled. Before the driver started his morning run, he would cover the bottom of the sled with hay to help keep the children warm.

But during the coldest winter days when the pupils arrived at school, they would complain, "Please, Teacher, my fingers and toes are frozen!"

"Let's get those frost-bitten fingers and toes warmed up," Teacher would say as she rubbed their hands and feet. "Then we'll begin class."

Long before John was old enough to go to school, he became familiar with the new building. Mama had taken John to special events at the school, including the fall fair. At the fair

74

Students at Hampton Consolidated, weeding the school gardens.

the students proudly displayed their handwriting, art work, woodworking, sewing, and fruits and vegetables they had grown in the school garden plots.

After missing a full year of school, seven-year-old John was now well enough to begin Grade 1. Mama was pleased to see how quickly John was learning to do things for himself. With only one arm, he had learned to get dressed, butter his own bread, and cut his meat with a fork. John found it was often the little things that were the hardest to do.

Sometimes John complained about not having two hands and wanting help.

His mother always replied, "John, you will need to discover, in your own way, how to do with one hand all the things that other people can do with two."

One evening in August, as Mama sat on the front veranda, she confided in Grandpa, "I'm thrilled that John is finally able to go to school with his friends!"

Evening Times-Globe

Saint John, N.B.   March 13, 1959

(Canadian Press)

"My mother was so wise in not pampering me," Humphrey recalls. "I learned to do the same things as other children – swimming, tennis and other sports – but I found my own way to do things."

75

Chapter *11*

The One-Armed Doukhobor

Primary classroom at Hampton Consolidated School, 1924.

"Tomorrow's a big day for you – your first day of school!" Mama said, as she tucked John into bed. "Good-night, my dear."

John tried to smile back at Mama. He didn't tell her he was scared to death. John tossed and turned most of the night, anxiously wondering what the kids at school would say about his missing arm.

"Will they make fun of me?" he worried.

The next morning before he left for school, John's mother carefully tucked the left sleeve of his shirt into the top of his pants. Mama hoped that having his sleeve tucked in would make his missing arm less noticeable. As he started out the door, Mama gave John a big hug. She, too, was concerned about how her son would manage at school.

John felt happy and safe walking to school with his older sister and brother. On the way, Ruth and Doug told John about school routines.

John's Gr.1 teacher, Miss Winnifred Dixon

"Every Monday and Friday we go to the Assembly Hall. It's up on the third floor," Doug explained. "The whole school marches into the hall, and Muriel – she's in Grade 10 – plays the piano."

"The principal reads from the Bible and then we all say the Lord's Prayer," Ruth added. "We always finish with a sing-song, and that's the best part!"

When the children arrived at school, John was eager to go to his classroom because he knew that the Grades 1 and 2 students were in the same room. John thought that was great, since he would be with his friends who were his age and now in Grade 2.

"Welcome," Miss Dixon smiled, as John stood at the entrance to the classroom. "You must be John Humphrey." John nodded shyly. "Come in and find a seat on the Grade 1 side, over by the windows."

John grinned as he spied Ralph and Douglas, sitting at desks on the Grade 2 side of the room.

Miss Dixon seemed friendly. All forty-eight pupils in the combined Grades 1-2 class soon grew to love her. John arrived home happy after his first day. He looked forward to returning.

It didn't take long for all the students in the school to know about the one-armed boy in Grade 1.

One day after Thanksgiving, two Grade 8 boys, named Murray and Charles, waited for John outside at recess time. These two had a reputation for being bullies. They led John away from the playing field to the side of the school.

John was scared because Murray and Charles were much older and bigger than he was. And they seemed mean.

Murray said, "Do you think Johnny can fight with just one arm?"

"Ha!" replied Charles, in a mocking voice, "Johnny's not a fighter!"

A crowd of boys came to watch, circling around John and his tormenters.

Charles loudly teased, "Diddle, diddle, dumpling, one-armed John; he went to bed with two arms on."

Murray encouraged the crowd to enter into the fun.

The other boys joined in, chanting, "Diddle, diddle, dumpling, one-armed John..."

Murray enjoyed exciting the crowd. "But when he woke up, his arm was chopped!"

Charles pantomimed a chopping action with his hand. The crowd hooted and they all repeated the chant together. John lowered his head so the boys couldn't see the tears running down his face. He didn't know what to do. If he ran they might chase him, or tease him worse the next time.

"Johnny, you can't fight Alan, can you?" Murray taunted.

John thought about what he should say. He tearfully replied, "I don't fight."

"Boo-oo!" the crowd yelled.

Ralph and Douglas rushed over to see what was going on. They watched from outside the circle of boys. They wanted to help John, but the other boys seemed so much bigger. As bad as they felt for him, John's good friends were too scared to speak up.

Charles and Murray started dancing around John, chanting, "John's a one-armed Doukhobor! John's a one-armed Doukhobor!"

The older pupils had learned in school that the Doukhobors were a religious group of people who had immigrated to Canada from Russia, and believed in a life of peace and goodwill. If the boys called you a Doukhobor, it was meant as an insult. You

Doukhobor family arriving in Saint John, New Brunswick, early 1900s.

were neither strong enough, nor brave enough, to stick up for yourself and fight back.

John was deeply hurt as the crowd chanted, "John's a one-armed Doukhobor!"

At the back of the school, John's older brother was playing ball with some of his friends. He heard the taunting and decided to see what was going on. Doug found John crouched on his knees, head down, surrounded by a group of boys. Charles was poking at John's empty sleeve with a stick. Doug was mad.

"STOP IT!" he yelled. "LEAVE MY BROTHER ALONE!"

Right behind Doug was a teacher who ordered the boys to stop immediately, and sent Charles and Murray to the principal's office.

As soon as the Humphrey children arrived home after school, John ran straight upstairs to his room.

"I'M NEVER GOING TO SCHOOL AGAIN!" he yelled, slamming the door to his room.

Doug and Ruth stayed in the kitchen to tell Mama what had happened.

"Poor John!" exclaimed Mama, broken-hearted.

John lay sobbing on his bed. "Now everyone in the whole world will tease me!"

Mama went upstairs and tried to comfort John.

"I'm sorry you were bullied. Those boys were very mean to you."

"I can't go back to school, Mama!"

"I don't think those bullies will tease you again. The principal will see to that."

"Those bullies were so mean! And all the other kids were laughing at me!"

"John, you have to go to school. If the bullies bother you again, tell Miss Dixon."

"NO, MAMA!" John started to cry.

"John, it's important to face your fears."

The next day, John reluctantly returned to school. He felt fine in the classroom but as soon as the recess bell rang, John was sure he was sick. Miss Dixon encouraged him to go outdoors and play with his friends.

As soon as John was outside, he ran to the field behind the school where his brother was playing.

Doug ran over and patted him on the head. "You'll be okay, John. Just yell if there's a problem."

From then on, even though Doug looked out for his little brother as much as he could, John was still teased from time to time.

John's Grade 2 year at school did not go well at all. He continued to suffer teasing. How he hated being picked on because he was different!

After school one day, as John sat on his bed, he finally decided, "Next time, I'm going to fight back." John punched his pillow. "Yes, I'll fight the bullies! I'll prove to them that I'm not a scaredy-cat! Maybe then, they'll stop picking on me."

The following day after school, John was picked on again. This time, he fought back furiously.

That evening as John stared at himself in his dresser mirror, he muttered, "No one's ever going to tease me again! I showed **them** how hard I can punch!"

John grimaced as he glared into the mirror at the face of a young boy, with a shiner on his right eye and a puffed-out upper lip!

Several weeks later, the principal of Hampton Consolidated shook his head in despair, as he finished writing a note to John's mother. As far as he was concerned, John was one of the two worst-behaved boys in the school!

November 15, 1913

Dear Mrs. Humphrey,

I regret to inform you that your son John was in another fight today. He needs to learn to control his temper; we have found him very difficult to manage over the past few weeks.

Yours truly,

Mr. C.T. Wetmore

Principal, Hampton Consolidated School

Mama was very upset when she read the principal's letter.
"Why is he getting into so much trouble?" she worried. "Is he still being bullied?"

Mama wondered how she should deal with John. She didn't know what to do. Mama wiped the tears from her eyes. It was time to go help her neighbour with the new baby.

"New babies are so much simpler," Mama sighed.

When Grandpa came downstairs, he noticed the letter from the principal on the kitchen counter. He was not pleased when he read it.

"That boy needs some discipline," muttered Grandpa. "And I better do it while Nellie's not here."

"John!" Grandpa ordered. "Out to the woodshed!"

Unbuckling his belt, Grandpa removed it from his pants and gave John a beating on his behind.

"That's a licking you won't forget in a hurry," Grandpa commented gruffly, as he slipped his belt back through the belt loops on his pants.

John cried, silently thinking, "I HATE GRANDPA. HE'S SO MEAN!"

But as deeply hurt as John was, he wouldn't have dared talk back to Grandpa. No one dared, except Mama, and she only occasionally argued with him.

By the next morning John had recovered his pride and returned to school. He was more careful to control his temper except when someone called him a "one-armed Doukhobor". Then he would fight back, no matter how big his tormenter was!

One day as John was coming home from school, two boys walked behind him and joked. "You know that one-armed boy, John Humphrey? I heard he lost his arm down the hole in the outhouse."

The other boy laughed, "Now that would be smelly!"

When John arrived home, he went upstairs to his room and flopped down on his bed. He just lay there and felt sorry for himself.

"It's not fair the way other kids pick on me. I'm not that different," he thought to himself.

It wasn't very long before Mama came upstairs to check on John. Seeing him so sad and knowing how many fights he had been in recently, Mama decided to tell him a story – one of Aesop's Fables.

The North Wind and the Sun

One day, the Wind and the Sun wanted to see which one of them was the stronger.

The Wind said to the Sun, "See that man down there? I will remove his cloak!"

The wind blew as hard as he could, but the man just wrapped the cloak more tightly around himself.

"This will be an easy game," the Sun laughed, shining as hard as he could, "and I shall be the winner."

Soon the traveler became so warm that he removed his cloak.

"See!" gloated the Sun.

"And that's how the gentle Sun outsmarted the forceful Wind," Mama concluded. "You see, John, using force does not solve problems. You have to be smart like the Sun, and find gentler ways to get what you want."

"What I want is to have people stop picking on me," John grumbled.

Mama patted his hand and went downstairs to prepare supper. John thought for a long time. Then he had an idea.

"Maybe I can learn to tie a bowtie. I know boys older than me who can't do that," he mused. "If I show them I'm as good as they are, then maybe they'll stop picking on me." Grabbing his blue-striped bowtie, he said with determination, "I can do this!"

John placed the tie around his neck, making sure that one end was longer than the other. He crossed the longer end over

It's hard to tie a bowtie!

the shorter end, bringing it up and over the loop, just like he had seen Doug do lots of times. Putting one end in his mouth, John pulled the other end tight with his right hand. Then he noticed that the longer end was too short to double over.

"Jeepers, this is hard!" he grumbled, as he sat down on his bed. "But, I'm no quitter!"

John pulled the tie loose, starting again. A half-hour later, he finally completed his bowtie. John gazed in the mirror; he didn't seem to notice that the bowtie was somewhat loose and a little lopsided.

"Better show Mama!" he grinned.

John marched downstairs, very proudly showing off his bowtie.

"I tied it all myself!"

Doug and Ruth clapped as John bowed.

"John, you're amazing!" said Mama, giving him a big hug. "I'm very proud of you!"

Hearing a knock at the back door, John ran to answer it. Ralph and Douglas wanted to play. John put on his coat and went outside. The boys had fun playing pirates. John pretended he was climbing the mast of the pirate ship, and went up as high as he dared in the apple tree, tightly hugging a branch with his one arm. As he looked down on his fellow pirates, he was reminded of what Mama had told him before his final surgery.

"Remember, your true friends will always be your good friends, no matter what."

Evening Times-Globe
Saint John, N.B.   March 13, 1959
United Nations, N.Y. (Canadian Press)
Canada's John P. Humphrey, a lanky 54, is best known for his gifts of intellect, but the things you notice first are the open smile, the easy friendliness…

"I never miss it [his left arm] – I can even knot a dress tie by myself," he said with a grin that seemed to mean he regards the handicap as an ever-stimulating challenge.

Chapter 12

Longing to be a Soldier

Grandpa rushed home from his usual stroll to the train station. It was the evening of August 4, 1914.

"Nellie!" Grandpa panted. "The station master told me William Barnes has received more news about the war in Europe. Germany has invaded Belgium!"

"Oh dear!" exclaimed Mama.

"There's talk it could lead to a world war!" Grandpa added, nervously.

Nine-year-old John, who was in the upstairs hallway, overheard their conversation.

"I'm not missing out on this!" he assured himself.

Sliding down the banister, John ran out the front door and down the street to Barnes' Store.

Canadian soldiers during The Great War.

A small group of people had gathered outside the window of the telegraph office. William Barnes was sitting in front of the teletype machine, waiting for more news. John felt his heart pounding with excitement. Suddenly, there was a hush. Everyone could hear the beeping of the Morse Code – another message coming through!

Mr. Barnes turned to the onlookers and commented, "Remember what Prime Minister Laurier said, *When Britain is at war, Canada is at war.*" Mr. Barnes nodded his head, "And he's right. Great Britain is our Motherland."

Everyone nodded in agreement and quickly walked home to spread the news.

John was thrilled. "Wow! A war! And I'm one of the first to know. This is the best day of my life!"

How John wished he were old enough to dress like a soldier and fight!

Two days following Britain's declaration of war, the training of Canadian soldiers began. In the next few months, thousands of families across Canada would be affected by the war, as teenage sons and young husbands left home to join the armed forces.

Canadian soldiers participating in physical training exercises at Camp Sussex, N.B.

Soldiers leaving Saint John for overseas, on the ship *SS Caledonia*, June 13, 1915.

In the Maritimes, after the soldiers received their military training, they sailed from either Saint John or Halifax, to Europe, where the fighting was taking place.

Trains travelling through Hampton Station always stopped long enough for the steam engines to take on water from the large water tank, located opposite John's house. While they waited, most passengers got off the train to stretch their legs.

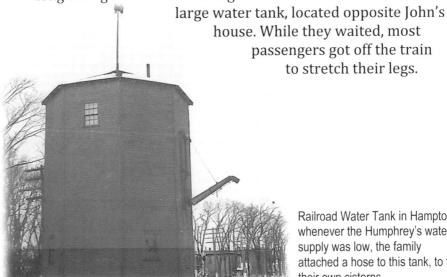

Railroad Water Tank in Hampton: whenever the Humphrey's water supply was low, the family attached a hose to this tank, to fill their own cisterns.

Every time a train stopped, John, now in Grade 3, ran over to the station platform to see if there were any soldiers. If there were, Mama let John take chocolates to offer them.

One November morning while passing the train station on his way to school, John saw the DeMille family. They were saying good-bye to their 22-year-old son, George, who was on his way to Nova Scotia for training. He was to become a soldier and travel overseas.

John stopped and watched while Mr. and Mrs. DeMille gave their son long hugs and repeated, "We love you, George. Take care of yourself."

"Why even George's father is crying," John puzzled, as he continued on to school.

Sadly, one and a half years later, George was killed in action overseas – by a "shell burst" at the Battle of Mont Sorrel in Belgium.

John felt really bad when he heard the news.

"I always thought it'd be fun to be a soldier," John confided later that day to Cousin Ralph. "But I never thought about getting killed."

George DeMille

Before being confronted with the awful reality of war, John had been envious of the soldiers who travelled through Hampton Station. All winter long, troops moved through Hampton, and John was usually there to greet them. He never tired of listening to the soldiers talk about The Great War, which eventually would be known as World War One.

One spring day, John saluted a young soldier who was standing on the station platform.

The other soldiers laughed, "I think you'd better wait a few years before you enlist in the army, young chap!"

During supper, John proudly announced, "Mama, a soldier let me try on his army hat!"

At bedtime, John fell asleep dreaming about soldiers.

That night, John was marching on the dock in Saint John, waiting to go onboard a ship that was on its way to Europe.

"SERGEANT HUMPHREY!" The General shouted. "Your gun, Sergeant! Where's your gun?"

"Here, sir!" replied Sergeant Humphrey, holding up a stick with a marshmallow on the end.

"SERGEANT HUMPHREY!" The General shouted again. "Your uniform is six sizes too big!"

Sergeant Humphrey tried to hide his baggy uniform by standing behind a much bigger soldier.

"Step out of line," commanded The General. "How old are you?"

"I'll be eighteen soon, General, Sir," Sergeant Humphrey lied, shaking in his boots.

"Are you ready for battle?" questioned The General fiercely.

"YES, SIR!"

"Then up the gangplank you go. FORWARD, MARCH!"

Sergeant John Humphrey lifted his short legs as high as he could, following a line of soldiers up the gangplank and onto the ship – destined for the war overseas.

"Left, right, left, right," John panted, swinging his legs and right arm high, until the sheets fell off the bed onto the floor.

"John, John," Mama said as she placed her hands on his shoulders.

John's legs still flailed in the air.

"John, it's alright," she repeated gently. "You're dreaming!"

John stopped marching and opened his eyes.

Mama smiled, "John, I have your favourite Saturday breakfast ready – fried eggs, pancakes and maple syrup!"

After breakfast John got dressed and went looking for Cousin Ralph. He had an idea how to make their army play more fun.

Chapter 13

Army Helmets for the Taking

Canadian Soldiers, in the Boer War era.

"Ralph," John sang out, spying his cousin down by the creek, "I heard my brother say there are army helmets in the attic of the Masonic Hall! They're left over from the Boer War!"

"Holy smoke!" replied Ralph, his jaw hanging open in disbelief and amazement.

"Let's go find them!" John grinned.

John and Ralph ran up the hill to the Masonic Hall. The boys then slowed to a walk as they cautiously moved to the back of the building.

After glancing around to make sure no one was watching, John nodded, "Let's go!"

Masonic Hall,
Hampton Station.

Once inside the back door, the boys saw another door which led to a small storage room.

Opening the inside door, Ralph whispered, "Hey, look at the ladder. It's nailed to the wall."

"See the boards," John murmured, pointing to the ceiling. "They're covering a hole. That must be the way to the attic!"

Ralph led the way up the ladder, lifted the boards and peeked inside. The attic was pitch black! Crawling into the attic the boys lay spread-eagle on the floor joists, reaching as far as they could with their arms.

"Holy Toledo!" whispered John. "I feel some helmets!"

"Me too!" Ralph giggled.

Piling all the army helmets they could find next to the opening, Ralph quickly climbed down the ladder.

"Catch, Ralph," John called as he tossed the helmets.

In their excitement, the boys forgot about being quiet.

"This is our lucky day!" Ralph laughed.

"What a great find!" John agreed.

"Catch, Ralph," John called as he tossed the helmets.

91

"Wait until our friends see the helmets!"

The local Masons were having a meeting that evening, with guests coming on the train from Saint John. Worshipful Master Mr. Flewwelling decided to make sure everything was in order for the meeting. Upon arriving at the Masonic Hall and opening the front door, Mr. Flewwelling thought he heard giggling.

"Children's voices?" Mr. Flewwelling wondered. "Coming from the storage room?"

Mr. Flewwelling walked softly across the floor of the main room and peeked around the door into the storage room. A boy stood at the bottom of the ladder, with his back to the door. He was trying to set a second helmet on top of the one already on his head. Another boy was starting to climb down the ladder. Noticing only one arm, Mr. Flewwelling knew immediately that the boy on the ladder must be John Humphrey.

"Wait until our friends see the helmets!" John said excitedly.

"Yeah, we're going to be very popular!" Ralph laughed, as he tried adding a third helmet on top of the other two.

"How popular do you think you'll be with the Masons?" Mr. Flewwelling asked, in a big harsh voice, swinging the door wide open.

John was so startled, he nearly missed the last two steps of the ladder. Ralph sheepishly turned around and faced Mr. Flewwelling, with a stack of three helmets teetering on his head.

It was all Mr. Flewwelling could do to keep from chuckling. He could imagine how much fun they were planning on having with the army helmets. Yet they were trespassing and stealing.

"Did anyone give you permission to take these helmets?" Mr. Flewwelling inquired, sternly.

"No," groaned the boys.

As the boys lowered their heads, John's helmet and Ralph's three helmets fell off and scattered on the floor.

Stole helmets

Trying not to laugh, Mr. Flewwelling asked, "You're Ralph March's son, aren't you?"

"Yes, sir," Ralph nodded.

"Are you boys aware that both your fathers were Worshipful Masters of this Lodge?"

John and Ralph both nodded, hanging their heads.

"John Humphrey, your father was a wonderful person – honest and respectful. He would not have approved of this misbehaviour! Ralph Junior, your father will not be happy to hear about your trespassing!" Mr. Flewwelling crossed his arms and slowly circled around the boys. "How old are you boys, and what grade are you in?"

"Ten, Sir; Grade 3, Sir," John replied.

"Almost ten, Sir; I'm in Grade 4, Sir," Ralph answered.

With lowered heads and trembling bodies, the boys feared what would happen next.

"I believe you meant no harm," Mr. Flewwelling nodded. "But, there needs to be a consequence for trespassing and taking things without permission."

While he scrutinized the boys, trying to decide on a punishment, Mr. Flewwelling assured them he would be letting their parents know about the incident.

"The Masons are having a meeting tonight. There will be a lot of cleaning up to do afterwards. Monday is Empire Day. As you are well aware, it is the anniversary of Queen Victoria's birthday, and we will be holding an evening celebration here. Come back on Monday and scrub the hall until it is spotless. That can be your punishment," Mr. Flewwelling decided, "if your parents agree to this."

The boys quickly nodded their heads. John sighed, thinking how much better this would be than a licking from Grandpa.

"Come early to clean," Mr. Flewwelling added, "so you'll be finished in time for the afternoon Empire Day Program at the school."

Early Monday morning, the boys arrived at the Masonic Hall. After they finished cleaning, the boys apologized to Mr. Flewwelling and promised never to trespass again.

"You seem to be good boys," Mr. Flewwelling replied, as he accepted their apologies. "These helmets are old and no longer of any use. I'll give them to you because your apology seems sincere and you have done a good job of cleaning the hall."

The boys thanked Mr. Flewwelling as he handed them the helmets. John and Ralph were overjoyed! They practically flew home, each wearing a helmet and carrying some more. The boys stored the helmets in John's family's shed.

John Humphrey

At age ten, John and Ralph had learned two valuable lessons – no trespassing and no stealing. These lessons would serve them well. In their adult years, John would work to protect human rights around the world, and Ralph would become Deputy Commissioner of the Federal Board of Penitentiaries (prisons) in Ottawa.

Ralph March

That afternoon at the Empire Day Program, John and Ralph excitedly told their friends about the army helmets. John invited them to come to his place on Saturday and play War Games.

Early Saturday morning, Ralph arrived at John's door and asked cautiously, "Do you think your mother would mind if we dug trenches in the backyard?"

"I think it will be fine with Mama," John replied. "But we can't dig near her garden… or Grandpa's apple orchard."

"I'll get extra shovels," Ralph offered, scurrying home.

The Humphrey's backyard was quite a sight that day - nine youngsters decked out in old army helmets, pretending to be soldiers. The boys loved hiding in the trenches they had dug. They imagined their sticks were real guns and that they were real soldiers. John was especially pleased because he played the part of General Humphrey!

Soldiers entering a trench, in France, during The Great War.

John's grade 4 teacher, Miss Howard, often talked to her students about The Great War. It was the fall of 1915 and the war had been going on now for over a year. In the December issue of *Punch* Magazine, Miss Howard found a poem written by a Canadian soldier. She asked all her students to memorize it. John would remember this poem for the rest of his life.

IN FLANDERS FIELDS

BY JOHN McCRAE

IN FLANDERS FIELDS THE POPPIES BLOW
BETWEEN THE CROSSES, ROW ON ROW,
    THAT MARK OUR PLACE; AND IN THE SKY
    THE LARKS, STILL BRAVELY SINGING, FLY
SCARCE HEARD AMID THE GUNS BELOW.

WE ARE THE DEAD. SHORT DAYS AGO
WE LIVED, FELT DAWN, SAW SUNSET GLOW,
    LOVED AND WERE LOVED, AND NOW WE LIE
    IN FLANDERS FIELDS.

TAKE UP YOUR QUARREL WITH THE FOE
TO YOU FROM FAILING HANDS WE THROW
    THE TORCH; BE YOURS TO HOLD IT HIGH
    IF YE BREAK FAITH WITH US WHO DIE
WE SHALL NOT SLEEP, THOUGH POPPIES GROW
    IN FLANDERS FIELDS.

Chapter *14*

Heartbroken

John's year in Grade 4 ended tragically. During the Christmas holidays, John noticed that Mama was often lying down. He wondered why but he didn't say anything.

Upon arriving home from school one day in January, John saw that there was no pot of cocoa on top of the wood stove. Mama always had cocoa waiting for them on cold winter days. Then he noticed that Mama was lying on the couch.

John's mother, Nellie Humphrey

"Mama, are you okay?" he asked. "Are you sick?"

Mama smiled and answered, "I'm alright John, just a little tired." She patted him encouragingly, "Now tell me about your day at school, and I'll make you some cocoa."

By the time John's 11th birthday came along in April, Mama hardly had enough energy to prepare meals. Seventeen-year-old Ruth made John's birthday cake.

Dr. Wetmore began dropping in to see Mama quite regularly. "Mrs. Humphrey," Dr. Wetmore informed her, "it's the cancer that's causing you to feel weaker. I'll come at the end of the week to check on you again."

One afternoon while Mama was lying on the couch, she beckoned for John to come and sit down beside her. Mama wanted to talk to him about something very important to her. She was finding it difficult to come up with the right words.

"John, I love you very much," Mama started. "And I want you to know, if anything should happen to me, I would like you to go to boarding school in Rothesay. You will get a good education there."

John hugged his mother, crying, "Mama, please don't die. I love you... I need you!"

With tears in her eyes, Mama hugged him long and hard.

Not long after that talk, and before the school year had finished, Mama became very weak. She spent most of her days in bed and was barely able to eat. Ruth did a lot to help around the house. Aunt Bessie was in and out several times each day, lending a hand. Mama's good friend, Jenny, often arrived with a dinner meal for the family.

Meanwhile, Grandpa wandered back and forth to the train station, worried about his lovely daughter, Nellie. After talking with Aunt Bessie on the telephone, Aunt Edith, Mama's sister who lived eight kilometers away in Central Norton, realized how seriously ill Mama was.

"I'll come tomorrow," Edith assured Bessie, "and I'll stay for as long as Nellie needs me."

On Sunday morning, Ruth, Douglas and John went to church, as usual. They knew Mama was too sick to go with them. Understanding how ill Mama was, Mrs. Rowley, the minister's wife, invited the children to come to her house after church for dinner.

Late in the afternoon, they returned home to find Dr. Wetmore's horse and carriage in the yard.

John's heart beat quickly. "Why is the doctor here again?" he asked nervously.

Uncle Leonard was on the front veranda talking quietly with Grandpa.

Dr. Wetmore's horse and carriage was in the yard again.

Dr. Wetmore, Aunt Bessie and Aunt Edith were upstairs with Mama. The house was practically silent. All you could hear was the soft opening and closing of doors, and whispering voices.

Before the children went to bed that night, they went into Mama's bedroom and gave her a kiss. Mama opened her eyes and gazed affectionately at each of her children – one last time.

"You mustn't stay too long," Aunt Bessie cautioned. "You don't want to tire out your mother."

John anxiously thought, "I don't want to leave Mama. She looks so sick. I might never see her again!"

With tears in his eyes, John finally, but reluctantly, returned to his bedroom.

As dawn broke, Mama stopped breathing. As soon as John awoke, Uncle Leonard went into his room.

"John, Mama is on her way to heaven to be with Papa. I'm very sorry."

John cried into his pillow for hours. All three children were devastated by the news, with no parents to comfort them. They found it hard to believe that Mama would no longer be there for them. By mid-morning, everyone in Hampton Station knew.

"Did you hear?" people quietly spoke. "Nellie Humphrey passed on early this morning."

Very quickly the women in the community started cooking for the family. For the next few days, there was a constant flow of neighbours and relatives in and out of the Humphrey's house. Everyone tried their best to be helpful and kind to the children.

Nellie's close friend, Jenny, prepared a beef stew for the family. When she delivered the stew, Ruth welcomed her to come in. Jenny smiled, expressed her sympathy, and sat in the front parlour with Ruth, Doug and John. Jenny recalled the good old days

"Poor John," Jenny said.

when she and Nellie had run in the fields together, chasing the cows and jumping over cow patties. Jenny tried to make John smile, with her stories of his mother picking flowers in the meadows and singing so sweetly in church.

Later, when John went outside to play with Ralph, Jenny moved into the kitchen to chat with a few neighbours. Nellie's next-door neighbour, Pauline, was setting the table.

"Poor John," Jenny said to Pauline. "Such a shame! He's too young to be without his mother!" She shook her head, remembering how strong Nellie had been after her husband died, ten years earlier. "And what a dear soul she was!"

"What on earth is going to happen to John?" Pauline asked, with concern.

A church-choir member, standing at the sink, interjected, "Surely his grandfather can't look after him!"

"That's for certain," agreed Pauline.

Looking around to make sure the children were not within earshot and that Grandpa was still out on the front veranda, Jenny whispered, "Thomas Peters is seventy-four, far too old and set in his ways to look after an 11-year-old! We just don't know what's going to happen to the children. But, my dears, I intend to find out!"

Just then the minister's wife, Mrs. Rowley, knocked on the back door to drop off some apple dumplings. As Mrs. Rowley was leaving, she saw John and Ralph out back by the apple trees. She called out to John, "If there's anything I can do to help... anything you want, John, please let me know."

John nodded politely but thought to himself, "The only thing I want is Mama back!"

John felt anger welling up inside him. He picked up a ball that was lying on the ground and threw it hard at one of the apple trees.

The following day, Mr. J.M. Scovil, the executor of Papa's will, arrived at the door. Mr. Scovil lived in a large farmhouse in Hampton Station which he had bought from Grandpa Peters, twenty-five years earlier. He was also one of the owners of Scovil Brothers' Clothing Store in Saint John. For many years, he and Papa had travelled together on the train into the city to work.

After expressing his sympathy to Grandpa over the loss of his daughter, and to the children on the loss of their mother,

Mr. Scovil sat down and talked with Ruth, Doug and John.

"John, your father requested that in case anything happened to your mother, while you were still young, I was to become your legal guardian."

John sat with his head bowed and listened, hardly believing that all this sadness was really happening.

"There is enough money from your father's life insurance to pay for the schooling of all three of you," Mr. Scovil continued. "The money will also be used to pay for a place for you to live."

"For how long?" Doug asked.

"Until you are old enough to look after yourselves," Mr. Scovil assured them.

Mr. Scovil once again expressed his sympathy and then left, promising to be in touch after the funeral.

For many nights, John cried himself to sleep. "I don't even remember Papa. Now I have no Mama!" He sobbed into his pillow. "I'm an orphan!"

After lunch on the day of Mama's funeral, Ruth spotted the Kings County Record on the kitchen counter. When she found Mama's obituary, she called her brothers. With tears running down their faces, they read it together.

THE KINGS COUNTY RECORD

SUSSEX, KINGS COUNTY, N.B.   JUNE 23, 1916   Price Two Cents

The Shiretown
[Hampton Station]

The death took place on Monday morning [June 19th] at five o'clock of Mrs. FM Humphrey, widow of the late FM Humphrey, who died in 1906. Mrs. Humphrey had been ill for some time and her death was not unexpected. She had a large number of friends and took an active part in church and social work. The funeral was held this afternoon at 3 p.m. from her late residence on Railway Avenue...

After Mama's funeral, Uncle Leonard took John aside and gave him a big hug. "Hold onto the many happy memories you have, John. Your mama was wonderful and very caring."

Leaning on Uncle Leonard, John started to sob.

As an adult, whenever John recalled his childhood, he thought of his mother. "I loved her deeply and she loved me. My mother gave me all the love that is so important in a child's life."

John's parents' tombstone, located in Hampton Rural Cemetery.

Chapter 15

Bullied at Boarding School

Students at Rothesay Collegiate School, about 1920.

After spending a sad and lonely summer without Mama, moving from one relative to another, the children got ready for fall. Doug, almost seventeen, stayed in Hampton with Aunt Bessie, so he could finish high school at Hampton Consolidated. Ruth, who'd be eighteen in October, would be moving to Sackville, New Brunswick, to attend Mount Allison University (Mount A).

Before she left, Ruth helped 11-year-old John get ready for boarding school.

"Let's take the train into Saint John, today," Ruth suggested, "and buy your school uniform."

John was excited with their purchase – a gray, military-looking uniform with black braid. He tried to persuade Ruth to let him wear it home on the train that day.

"No, John," Ruth said very definitely. "You'll have to wait until next week, when you're at boarding school."

A few days after Ruth had left for Mount A, John wrote her a letter. He still used his special nickname for Ruth.

Dear Rufus,

I've missed you since you left last Saturday. I miss Mama very much.

Last night I had a dream. I was running in our back door and Mama was in the kitchen. She smiled at me. Then she put cookies in the oven. It seemed so real. I tried to hug her but I couldn't reach her.

Doug told me he wants to work at a bank when he graduates from Hampton Consolidated. Did you know that?

Aunt Bessie helped me pack my trunk yesterday. On Thursday, Mr. Scovil will go on the train with me to Rothesay Collegiate. I can hardly wait. I think I'll like it there. Wish me good luck.

Do you like it at Mount A? Is university fun?

John

Rothesay Collegiate School (RCS) was a private boys boarding school in the town of Rothesay – a forty-five minute train-ride from Hampton, en route to Saint John.

When John arrived at RCS, the principal of the school, known as The Headmaster, greeted him.

"Welcome to Rothesay Collegiate, Humphrey," Rev. Hibbard said, briskly.

John learned that Rev. Hibbard had a nickname. Behind his back, the students called him The Beak – so named because of his long nose, curved like the bill of a hawk. John would soon discover that The Beak had a very bad temper.

Whenever new boys arrived at the boarding school, they were "christened" by being thrown into the brook. It was part of being new to the school.

As the boys threw John into the brook, someone called out, "There goes Fatty."

"Am I really fat?" John wondered later that day, staring at his image in a mirror. "Or is it just the way this uniform hangs on me?"

As an adult, John wrote in his unpublished autobiography:

"I have some pleasant memories of Rothesay Collegiate, but not many...

I couldn't keep my uniform neat; it bulged where it should not have and my stockings (I was still wearing short pants) had a way of sliding down my legs.

My worst enemy was my own temper, which I made little effort to control and which was only too easily provoked."

The next day as John walked to class, one boy called out to him "Hi Fatty!"

Another boy snickered, "Oh, there's Fatso!"

John became very upset whenever the other boys called him names and made fun of his missing arm.

Several weeks later when John was returning from the dining hall, he heard someone behind him say, "If it isn't the one-armed Doukhobor!"

John turned around and punched the boy in the nose.

"I HATE RCS!" John yelled, as he ran back to his room in the boys' residence.

John's worst enemy was his own temper. Being called a one-armed Doukhobor always sent him into a fury.

Strangely enough, when John was a baby, his family often called him The Duke, because his big nose reminded them of Queen Victoria's son, the Duke of Connaught.

Remembering the old family nickname, John admitted, "I like it when my friends call me The Duke. Why can't the bullies do that?"

Boarding school was a big change for John. Having left Hampton Consolidated and all his friends behind, he felt anxious about being accepted in a new place, especially after the "christening" incident! In Hampton, students had learned to accept John for who he was – an adventurous, fun-loving boy – rather than the boy with the missing arm. At boarding school, the students regarded him as the boy who was different, an easy target for bullying. For John, it felt like he was starting all over again!

"I wish I were in Grade 5 in Hampton. It'd be so much more fun there," John sighed as he thought of his friends back home. "They wouldn't like it here either. They'll never believe me when I tell them how the Masters watch us like hawks when we do homework!"

On week-nights after supper, RCS students returned to their classrooms. The classrooms were divided into cubicles by glass partitions. John always sat in the same cubicle. Each night, a Master Teacher stepped up on the high throne, located in the hall. From there, he could survey all the students.

"Study class will begin," the Master spoke, with great authority. "You will only read from textbooks and there will be NO TALKING, until you hear the gong at nine o'clock."

When John got tired of studying, he often sketched. "Someday, when I'm older," he dreamed, "I want to be a cartoonist."

John's school books were full of sketches, like the drawing in the back of his *Natural History* textbook. John refrained from titling it "The Beak", in fear the Headmaster might see it and he'd get in trouble!

Sketch drawn by John, in his textbook.

Each week-day morning, there was a chapel service led by Rev. Hibbard, who was a very powerful speaker. Knowing how important it was not to fidget while the Reverend was speaking, the boys did their best to sit still. No one wanted to get into trouble with The Beak.

On Sundays it was compulsory for all students to attend church service, held at the Anglican Church in Rothesay. In Grade 6, John blew the bugle in the cadet band that led the parade of students from the school over to the church.

"Playing a bugle is the only role in the parade appropriate for a one-armed boy," the director of the band, Sergeant Dooey, had said.

"I'm not very good at playing the bugle," John remarked to his roommate one Sunday morning as he put on his starched white collar. "But, what the heck! I've learned to play a few songs. Besides, I get to march at the front of the parade!"

Back row, far right: John holding a bugle in the Cadet Corps.

Back row:
Mr. C.T. Wetmore,
principal and coach.
Middle row, far left:
Jack Angevine,
brother of John's
friend, Douglas.
Front row, far right:
John's brother, Doug.

Track Team at Hampton Consolidated School, 1917.

John had many days at RCS when he was lonely. When the mail arrived, he felt sad watching the other boys receive letters from their mothers. John was thankful that Rufus and Doug wrote to him so at least he received some mail.

Dear John,

Sorry I haven't written in a while. How are you? Is grade six better than last year?

Our school won the Kings County Track Meet two weeks ago. I placed first in the high jump and we placed second in the track relay.

Here is a photo of our team with the trophy. Be careful of the photo. I want it back the next time I see you.

Let's go to a movie, maybe next week-end.

Doug

"It would be fun to go to a movie with Doug," John thought, as he looked at the photo, recognizing most of the boys.

Suddenly, John felt very homesick for Hampton.

"If Mama were still alive," John wished desperately. "I wouldn't have to be here!"

Although John had made a few friends at boarding school, the bullies still pursued him, looking for opportunities to tease him. John hated being bullied. He also hated the harsh discipline from the Masters. Most of them gave lickings to the boys when they misbehaved. Feeling particularly angry one Sunday after church, John wrote to Ruth.

> *Dear Rufus,*
>
> *At church parade this morning, the Sergeant reported a lot of fellows to The Beak. I was one of them for not having black boots on. I haven't got any now.*
>
> *I didn't have a hard collar on either. Gee. We have to pay out of our own money to get our collars cleaned.*
>
> *The Beak will call us up by Monday.*
>
> *John*

During John's first two years at RCS, the Great War was continuing to rage in Europe. At home in Canada there was a constant appeal for more food.

In the spring of 1918, students at the boarding school helped out with the war effort by working on Mr. Fairweather's farm located nearby. On Saturday mornings 13-year-old John, as part of a group of twenty boys, would climb into the back of a truck and head for the farm.

When they arrived, John sighed with pleasure, "It's good to be working outside."

With hand-saws, hoes and shovels, the boys formed a work gang and cleared land so that more food could be grown. After they had been working for a couple of hours, John stumbled just as the boy beside him thrust his shovel toward the hard ground. Instead of digging into the soil, the shovel cut into John's left leg. John let out a yelp.

"My leg! It's bleeding!"

The driver of the truck quickly took off his sweater and wrapped it around John's leg to stop the bleeding. Helping him into the cab of the truck, the driver drove John to the doctor.

"That's a nasty gash," Dr. Peters confirmed, as he cleaned the wound and prepared his needle and thread... "There you go, John – those stitches should do it. You'd better wait a while before clearing any more land."

At the end of each day, the boys were paid some for their labour. Most of their earnings, however, went to the Red Cross. They in turn sent food parcels overseas to prisoners-of-war.

In John's third year at RCS, even though he still disliked boarding school, he enjoyed going to the library. Now in Grade 7, John had developed a love of reading. On one of his many visits to the library, he sat at a table and wrote Ruth a letter.

'Rufus',
writing a letter.

Dear Rufus,

Thanks for the poetry books. I enjoy reading them.

I've discovered that I have as good a brain as any of my classmates. Two weeks ago, I wrote an essay advocating the union of the three Maritime Provinces. Do you know what Uncle Percy did? He had it published in the Saint John Telegraph!

What do you think of your little brother having something published in the newspaper?

I think Mama would be pleased, don't you?

John

Ruth was proud of John. The following week, she wrote him back.

Dear John,

Congratulations! Mama would be very pleased!

Last month, you wrote telling me you wanted to run away from RCS. I know you don't like it there. I'm sorry John, but I can't do anything about that. Mr. Scovil is the only one who can.

I talked to a friend here at Mount A, whose brother is at RCS. His name is Gordon. He's a year older than you are, but is willing to share his room with you. Let me know how you feel about this.

Rufus

John liked the idea. "Gordon's a good athlete, and he's popular," John smiled.

With the help of Uncle Percy Humphrey who spoke to The Headmaster, John was allowed to move to Gordon's room.

When Gordon's friends asked him about his new roommate, he replied, "John's a funny kid – quite a temper. But he's smart and has lots of spirit. You soon forget he only has one arm because he does almost everything."

John and Gordon often sat together for meals in the dining hall. As John joked with Gordon, he watched with delight while two of the school bullies, seated at the next table, stared in their direction.

"How did Fatty Boy get to be Gordon's buddy?" one of the bullies grumbled.

"Hey," John grinned, "when I'm with Gordon, I'm safe."

Sticking out his chest, John sat up straight on the edge of his chair, feeling a new sense of confidence. But John still didn't feel safe meeting up with the bullies when he was alone.

Whenever John had free time, he went hiking in the woods behind the school. In the winter John trapped for hares and would go every day after school to check his traps. One day, John headed to the woods with his friend Carl, who loved the outdoors as much as he did.

"Wow!" John said in amazement, as he checked his last trap. "I've caught six hares today."

"What are you going to do with them?" asked Carl.

"I'm taking them to the school kitchen."

The cook greeted the boys at the door. "Thank you, John. I'll make rabbit stew, enough for everyone."

"I hope the boys like the stew!" John murmured. "If the bullies don't like it and they find out I provided the hares, I'll be in big trouble!"

The next day at supper, John was relieved to see the school bullies wolfing down the stew. One of them even asked for seconds.

Although money was tight, John saved up to buy a bicycle.

"Hey, Carl!" John called out. "Look at the second-hand bike I bought. Isn't it a beauty!"

"Looks great," Carl replied.

"Now I can bike into Saint John and visit Uncle Percy." John sighed as he remarked, "It's the closest thing I have to a home."

Whenever John visited Uncle Percy and Aunt Nell, he had fun playing with his cousins. He was fascinated with the water-colour canvasses his older cousin Jack painted.

Sometimes John rode his bike, without permission, to Saint John. The students were easy to spot in their school uniforms. John, with only one arm, was particularly easy to recognize.

One day a woman called the school.

"Rev. Hibbard," the woman said, "it may be none of my business but I saw that one-armed boy biking toward the city this afternoon."

"Ah, that's one of the Grade 7 boys. Thank you, madam, for your call," Rev. Hibbard replied.

Upon his return, John got word he was wanted in The Headmaster's office. Fearfully, John knocked on The Beak's office door.

"Come in, Humphrey. Stand right there," The Beak ordered, pointing his finger to a spot on the floor.

Opening the center drawer of his desk, The Beak pulled out a black leather strap. John reluctantly held out his right hand.

"WHACK, WHACK..." eight whacks altogether. John flinched but he was determined not to cry.

"This is for leaving the school without permission," said Rev. Hibbard, taking his temper out on John's hand. "Disobedience will not be tolerated at RCS, Humphrey! You are dismissed."

John left The Beak's office with a welt rising on his right hand.

Walking back to the boys' residence, John muttered passionately,

"I'm going to find a way out of here! NO WAY am I staying at RCS!"

Chapter 16

Celebrating the Victory

Dining hall at RCS, about 1920.

November 11, 1918, was a day that 13-year-old John would always remember. It was a Monday morning and the boys were in the dining hall eating their breakfast. John was pouring molasses on his porridge when the Headmaster appeared. A hush spread across the room.

As the Headmaster said, "Good morning, Gentlemen," the boys scrambled to their feet and stood at attention.

"Good morning, Rev. Hibbard, Sir," replied the boys, in unison.

"I have very important news this morning," Rev. Hibbard announced. "The War is over! We will celebrate the victory!"

Everyone was elated! The Great War was finally over. It had seemed like a long four years, especially to the boys who were waiting for their fathers or older brothers to return home from overseas.

Victory Parade
in Saint John.

To celebrate the end of the war, the Headmaster ordered extra food for a party. The students spent the day building a bonfire. In the evening when the bonfire was lit, the blaze was visible for many kilometers around.

"Holy Cow! This bonfire is as big as a house!" John said to his friend Carl. "And look at all the sandwiches and cookies The Beak has given us!" John raved, drinking another bottle of soda pop.

The next day, the Headmaster arranged for several trucks to pick up the students and take them to Saint John for a victory parade. The boys were excited as they watched the parade going down King Street. Everyone cheered as the soldiers passed proudly by. John could hardly believe his eyes.

"This is the biggest parade ever!" John exclaimed. "I'll never forget this!"

Parade on King Street in Saint John, 1918.

Chapter 17

John Plans his Escape

Students in front of RCS School House, 1920.

The day following the parade, life at RCS returned to normal. John was back to hating boarding school. He was also desperate for some spending money.

One morning John had a stroke of good luck. On his way to breakfast, he saw a new boy at the school closing all the windows along the middle floor of their residence.

John asked him, "Do you get paid for doing that?"

The new boy nodded.

"How much?"

"Twenty-five cents a week."

"I could do that for you, and you could sleep in an extra fifteen minutes," John coaxed. "Deal?"

"Alright. Only for a week."

"I'll start tomorrow," John declared happily as the boys shook hands.

John soon spent the extra money. How he wished he could have kept the job of closing the windows! Whenever he felt sorry for himself, John would write Ruth a letter.

Dear Rufus,

I had to borrow this stamp. Just by luck I got it too. Say, Rufus, next letter you send me you might drop in two stamps. I busted a window so I won't get any pocket money next week. Gee, it's hard luck...

Well, Rufus, there's absolutely nothing to talk about at this old school – the same thing happens every day except when you break a window – why in hang don't they make windows that don't break anyway?

John

Like the other students, John found the residence very cold in winter. Sometimes when he wrote to Ruth, he jokingly headed his letter with another name for RCS.

Rothesay Cold Storage

Dear Rufus,

I'm not getting along good with the headmaster at all. There's a new rule every day and that's no exaggeration. Lights go out at half-past nine. Gee, but I long for the holidays... They're trying to make it into a sort of reform school. Why, if you're even late for [church] parade, they will give you a licking.

John

"A licking?" sighed Ruth, shaking her head sadly. "Being beaten with a belt sounds terribly severe. I wish I could help him, but I can't. I'm not his guardian."

Now in his fourth year of boarding school, 14-year-old John could think of little else other than leaving RCS.

"I've got to come up with an escape plan," John determined, as he went for his usual walk in the woods. "I know Mr. Scovil won't approve of my leaving. He thinks I'm here for another four years. But I don't care. I am not coming back next year!"

A favourite winter pastime was skating outdoors on New Brunswick's frozen rivers and creeks.

During the Christmas holidays, John spent time in Hampton at his cousin Ralph's house. One day while he was skating on Ossekeag Creek, John met his friend Douglas, who had been with him that awful day of the fire in the outhouse. Douglas was with his older brother Jack who was in his final year of high school.

When John told the boys how unhappy he was at RCS, Jack suggested, "John, why don't you write the same Provincial High School Exams I plan to write, come summer?"

"That sounds like a crazy idea!" laughed John.

"But if you pass them," Jack countered, "then you can apply to university."

"It might be my only way out," John reflected. "I'll think about it," he replied.

John and Douglas skated around the creek together, catching up on each other's recent adventures.

"If you want to try it," Jack called out, whizzing by, "I'll loan you some textbooks."

It was dusk when the boys finished skating.

John was perplexed. "It would be a lot of hard work," he admitted to himself, "and probably take a lot of good luck for me to pass."

It was dusk when the boys finished skating. As John untied his skates, a decision became clear to him.

"If passing the Provincial Exams will make it so I can leave RCS," John resolved, "then I'll give it my best shot!"

"Jack," he called out, "I'll come by your house for some books before I go back to RCS. And thanks," John smiled.

For the next six months, John studied long hours, in secret. He took a book with him everywhere he went, even to the toilet!

During his summer holiday at Ononette, John didn't study as hard. There were too many fun things going on. At fifteen, John had a new interest – girls – an intriguing experience for him, having spent the last four years at an all-boys boarding school.

Chapter *18*

Adventures on the St. John River

At Ononette, John learned to swim.

Ever since Mama's death, Ruth, Doug and John had spent their summers together at Ononette, on the St. John River. Although Mr. Scovil paid for them to stay in rented rooms, they also spent a lot of time at Uncle Percy and Aunt Nell's summer home.

John had learned to swim at Ononette, the first summer after Mama had died. He'd spent many hours in the water practising, and eventually discovered that what worked best for him was his own version of a sidestroke.

The summer that John was fifteen, he decided to teach himself to play tennis.

"It'll be a nice break from studying for Provincials," John told himself. "I'll come here early tomorrow. That way I'll learn to hit the ball before anyone else gets here. I can borrow a racket from Uncle Percy."

The next morning, John arrived at the tennis court at six o'clock. He held the ball and racket together in his one hand and murmured thoughtfully, "If I throw the ball up really high, I'll have time to get a good grasp on the racket."

John threw the ball high into the air, swung his racket, and missed. Again and again he tried, but failed. Although he was

117

getting discouraged, John kept throwing the tennis ball up in the air because he was determined he could do it. Finally the ball and racket connected and John smashed the ball across the net.

"I did it!" John shouted. "Wait till my friends see!"

At Ononette, the St. John River was about a kilometer wide. Anxious to experience the wind on the sails, John decided to rent a small catboat with a red sail. On his first venture out, Uncle Percy and Doug watched from shore.

Uncle Percy was flabbergasted. "Doug, do you see that? John has the rope between his teeth!"

"It looks like he's controlling the tiller by sitting on it," Doug laughed.

"That nephew of mine is very ingenious," admired Uncle Percy, "and adventurous!"

One Saturday night John's cousins, Uncle Percy's sons, persuaded him to go dancing at the Country Club.

John enjoyed being around girls, although he felt a little awkward when he was with them. After watching on the side-lines for most of the evening, John finally got up enough courage to ask a girl, named Mary, to dance. He'd seen her swimming at the wharf. Quickly wiping the sweat off his hand, John went over to where Mary was standing.

"Do you want to dance?" he asked, shyly.

Mary smiled and took John's hand. They moved onto the dance floor where she put her right hand on his left shoulder.

John kept an eye on the girls swimming at the wharf.

John returned often to enjoy the girls' campfire and singsong.

As they danced, John did his best not to step on her feet!

John later confided in his cousins, "I liked dancing, but I was really nervous. I couldn't think of anything to say to her. We smiled at each other a lot!"

After that, John looked forward to the Saturday night dances and was much braver about asking girls to dance.

On the other side of the river from Ononette was Sand Point, a place where a group of girls from Fredericton came every summer to camp. John was very interested in getting across the river to visit them. On his first paddle to their campsite, one girl named Doris watched in amazement.

"Look, girls!" Doris cried out. "That young chap is paddling towards our beach... with the end of the paddle under his chin!"

"I think he has only one arm!" exclaimed another.

John returned often to enjoy the girls' campfire and singsong. One evening, a strong wind came up. Doris was worried.

"The water has turned very rough, John. What are you going to do?"

John answered nonchalantly, "I'll spend the night on the beach."

John smiled at the girls while they giggled and watched him make himself comfortable. In a very short time, John had prepared a make-shift bed underneath his overturned canoe.

Chapter *19*

Too Young?

John, at age 15, in academic robe at Mount Allison University.

In August, 15-year-old John took the train from Ononette to Saint John, to write the Provincial High School Exams. Each day thereafter, John went to Uncle Percy's summer home and scanned the newspaper for exam results. Finally, John saw the headline – *Local Students Pass Provincial Exams*. He anxiously read down the list, looking for his name.

Jumping up excitedly, John let out a loud, "Yahoo!"

Immediately John grabbed pen and paper to jot a note to Ruth. (Ruth had just received a teaching position in Montreal and was getting settled into a new apartment there.)

Dear Rufus,
  I'm very happy today! I passed the provincial exams!
John

Ruth wrote back.

> *Dear John,*
>
> *Congratulations, dear brother. You are amazing!*
> *Your sister, and friend always,*
>
> *Rufus*

In his next letter, John wrote:

> *Rufus,*
>
> *I have more good news. I've been accepted at Mount A. I suppose it helped having Uncle Lawrence there as a professor. [Professor Killam was married to Papa's sister, Edith, a well-respected painter.] Oh, I know; it likely helped my chances that you just graduated from there with high honours.*
>
> *Even if strings were pulled to have me accepted, it's okay. I'm happy.*
>
> *John*

Ruth thought John was far too young to go to university and told him so in her letter. John wrote a quick reply:

> *Rufus,*
>
> *I think you're mighty discouraging. I'm not too young to go to Mount A.*
>
> *John*

Mr. Scovil was astounded that John had passed the Provincial Exams, and amazed that he had been accepted at Mount A. Although Mr. Scovil was doubtful that John was mature enough to go to university, he forwarded the money to Mount A.

"After all," he sighed, "I made an agreement with Frank many years ago to use the insurance money for his children's education."

In September, 1920, John was busy getting ready to move to Sackville. He was excited about going to Mount A. Before he left, John asked Uncle Percy to go shopping with him.

Uncle Percy and Uncle Guy, wearing fedoras (fashionable felt hats).

121

Men's residence at Mount A, 1920.

Dear Rufus,

    Everything is great here. I'm living on the fourth floor of the men's residence. My room is along the corridor known as hell's alley. There are lots of pranks being pulled here.

    Mount A is so much better than RCS.

John

"I want to buy a new suit and a nice soft fedora, like the ones you and Uncle Guy wear. I want to look good when I arrive on the train!"

Soon after arriving at Mount A, all the first-year students had their photos taken in academic robes, as members of the graduating class of 1924. John, however, was not destined to graduate from Mount A.

"Oh dear," Ruth said regretfully as she read John's letter. It was the first she had heard from him since he'd moved to Mount A. "I have a feeling John's not doing very well," Ruth sighed. "I don't think he's doing any studying!"

Mount A was very different from RCS – no study hall at night, and no Masters giving lickings for bad behaviour. Since university students were expected to be mature and responsible, they were given more freedom. John abused this new sense of freedom by playing most of the time, and doing very little school work.

Having arrived back at his residence after class one afternoon, John found a box of home-baked goodies in his mailbox, from Aunt Nell and Uncle Percy. John and his friends enjoyed the treats. The following week, he wrote Aunt Nell to thank her.

Dear Aunt Nell,

    Thanks for the box. It certainly did go to the right spot. We are still eating marmalade and toast...

    At Thanksgiving, a crowd of us got together and hired a car and went to Moncton to see the game there. You should have seen the car, no brakes, no lights, poor steering gear, rotten gears, etc. We had everything happen to it that could possibly happen to a car. It was even on fire and we bumped into a big Studebaker in Moncton!

John

Mount A students, beside a model T car, early 1920s.

Uncle Percy wrote back and reminded John not to forget about studying. But John seemed to ignore this advice.

"Hey, boys!" John called out one evening as he held a water balloon out his residence window. "Here comes another victim! Watch this!"

John dropped the water balloon and the boys shrieked with laughter. A young woman, who was passing by on the path below, was soaked.

Another day, John chummed along with some boys who took a pig from the college farm, greased it, and put it in the university chapel! The authorities never found out who did it.

John seemed to be enjoying himself at Mount A. But at fifteen, he had no idea what he wanted to do with his life. As a result, he had no incentive to work. A trip to Montreal changed John's mind and gave him a new goal to strive toward.

Chapter 20

Christmas in Montreal

Montreal, corner of St. Catherine and Stanley Streets, 1915.

"Look at us, Doug," mused John, as they made their way to Ruth's place, "riding an electric streetcar in downtown Montreal!"

It was during John's second year at Mount A that he went to visit Ruth in Montreal. Now a 23-year-old high school teacher, Ruth had invited her two brothers to come visit her over the Christmas holidays. Doug had just turned twenty-two, and John was sixteen.

"Thanks for inviting us, Rufus," John said, smelling his favourite molasses cookies. "That's a nice little Christmas tree," he nodded.

"Hey, those look like our old Christmas ornaments," Doug remarked. "John, do you remember that one with the silver sparkles?" he asked, pointing to a top branch.

"Yeah," John replied. "There were two of them, except I broke one – by accident, of course!"

John winked at Doug, remembering when Doug had tossed the ornament in his direction and he'd missed catching it.

Ruth smiled, remembering all the mischief her brothers used to get into.

"Those look like our old Christmas ornaments."

"I'm so glad to see both of you!" she replied, hugging them.

John and Doug each gave her a peck on the cheek and a quick hug in return.

"On our way from the train station," John remarked, "I was surprised to see a man with only one arm. You know, it hardly ever occurs to me that I present the same picture to other people."

While they had tea and cookies, John recalled his first visit to the big city.

"It's been nearly ten years since I was in Montreal with Uncle Leonard."

"I remember that well," remarked Doug. "Mama was very upset when you and Uncle Leonard returned home."

Ruth nodded, remembering how Mama had cried when Uncle Leonard told her that the Montreal doctors couldn't save John's arm.

"All I remember," said John, reminiscing, "was the grand Windsor Hotel... and room service. I was so excited when they delivered supper to our room. As I recall," John laughed, "I complained to Uncle Leonard about too much pepper on the corn."

John and Doug had a good visit with Ruth. They explored the city and had lots of time to chat.

Three days into their stay, John decided that he loved Montreal and told Ruth, "I'm going to find a way to move here."

"Perhaps you could study at McGill University," Ruth suggested.

"But how can I convince Mr. Scovil to send me to McGill?" he wondered aloud.

John knew that Mr. Scovil wanted him to become a businessman, like his father and grandfather had been. Mr. Scovil had already convinced Brother Doug to go into business.

"I know what I can do," John announced to Ruth. "In order for Mr. Scovil to approve my moving to Montreal, I'll study Business at McGill."

"Yes, that might just work," Ruth smiled, slowly. "And you can tell Mr. Scovil that I'll be nearby to keep an eye on you!"

Several years after John and Doug's visit to Montreal, Doug married Gertrude Ewing. They had one child.

Doug, with his wife Gert, and baby Gail.

Chapter **21**

John Falls in Love

John moved to Montreal the following September. Although he was only seventeen, this time he studied and did well. After earning a degree in Business, John decided to study Law, which he found especially interesting. In 1929, when John graduated with his Bachelor of Civil Law degree, he received a scholarship.

"Imagine a year of studying Law in Paris!" John grinned. "This will be a great way for me to learn more about International Law, and to improve my French at the same time."

Now 24 years old, John travelled to France on an ocean liner. The first

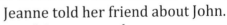
John graduates from McGill University.

evening after the ship had set sail, John went to a dance. It was there he noticed a pretty young woman from Montmagny, Quebec, named Jeanne Godreau.

"Maybe I'll ask her to dance," John thought.

Jeanne agreed to dance with him. When she returned to her cabin, Jeanne told her friend about John.

Jeanne Godreau

"He seems to be a very likeable young man. If truth be known, I might be in love!"

John and Jeanne spent most of their time on board ship together.

"You speak French extremely well," admired Jeanne. "Did you really grow up in an English-speaking village, *au Nouveau-Brunswick, mon cheri* (in New Brunswick, my dear)?"

To other passengers on board, it looked like John and Jeanne had fallen in love!

"I'm sorry, but I'll be leaving the ship in England for a short stop-over," John told Jeanne. "I want to visit my sister Ruth. She's studying at Oxford University. But I'll be travelling on to Paris, soon, my dear."

On their last night together, John and Jeanne were leaning against the rail on the upper deck. It was a beautiful starry night.

"Jeanne," John said. "I love you. Will you marry me?"

Jeanne smiled and kissed him, but she didn't answer his question.

The next morning the ship docked in England, and John disembarked as planned. While waiting at the train station, John sent Jeanne a telegram.

EASTERN TELEGRAPH COMPANY
EUSTON STATION, ENGLAND

RECEIVED AT __ 10:50 A.M.   DATED__ June 21, 1929

TO__ MLLE. JEANNE GODREAU
    ON BOARD SHIP AURANIA
    ENGLISH CHANNEL

Jeanne, Please marry me, John.

Ruth was looking forward to John's visit. It had been over a year since she had seen him. Ruth answered a knock at the door.

"Telegram, madam," said the messenger. "It's for Mr. John Humphrey."

Ruth thanked the young man and returned to preparing fish chowder, one of John's favourite dishes.

As Ruth finished in the kitchen, she glanced out her front window and saw John sprinting up the walkway.

"John," Ruth said, giving him a hug, "I'm so glad you've come!"

When John saw the telegram on the table, he asked nervously, "Rufus, is that for me?"

"Yes it is," Ruth smiled, curious about how anxious John appeared.

John, with his sister, Ruth.

John ripped open the telegram and quickly read the message. It was from Jeanne. Her reply was one word – *Oui* (yes).

After carefully tucking the telegram into his pocket, John announced, "Rufus, the love of my life has said she'll marry me! I'm sorry," John apologized, "but I must leave tomorrow so I can be with Jeanne in Paris."

In September, Ruth travelled to France to attend John and Jeanne's wedding. The priest at the church where they had wanted the wedding, wouldn't marry them, because John refused to become a Roman Catholic.

Somewhat discouraged, Jeanne spoke to John. "I know it's very important to my parents that I be married in a church. Is there anything we can do?" she asked.

"I know how we might solve that problem," John replied, with a twinkle in his eye.

After the wedding ceremony, held at the British Embassy (there was no Canadian embassy in Paris at the time), John and Jeanne walked to the nearest Catholic Church, and Ruth took their picture. Jeanne sent the photo to her parents in Quebec, with a note on the back, saying:

> *John and Jeanne on the church steps, after they were married.*

Jeanne's parents never discovered that Jeanne and her new husband John Humphrey had not been married **inside** the church!

John, with his wife, Jeanne.

Chapter 22

A Great Moment in History

United Nations Emblem: the world, surrounded by two olive branches (a symbol of peace).

When John finished his studies in Paris, he and Jeanne returned to Montreal where John worked as a lawyer for six years. This was during the 1930s – a decade known as The Great Depression – when many people had no job and therefore, no money.

In the mornings, on his way to work at the law office, John would shake his head, "Look at the people on the streets, struggling to survive. Every day there's a long line-up at the soup kitchen. These people are desperate. How can they be helped?" he wondered.

Soup kitchen in Montreal, during the Depression.

In 1936, in the midst of the Depression, John began teaching Law at McGill University. John, now Professor Humphrey, had a special interest in International Law.

John and Jeanne in their Montreal apartment.

Ten Years Later

In 1946, 41-year-old John, now Dean of Law at McGill, received a long-distance call from Henri Laugier – an old friend he had met in Montreal a number of years earlier. Monsieur Laugier was the Assistant Secretary-General of the United Nations, in New York City.

"You're asking me to be the Human Rights Director at the United Nations?" John asked, in awe.

"What an opportunity!" he reflected to himself. "I'd meet people from around the world who'd be interested in discussing world peace... but I'd miss teaching...yet..." John paused. "I'll check with Jeanne and call you back."

John and Jeanne sat down and talked about leaving Montreal and moving to New York. They had no children; so they didn't need to be concerned about moving children away from school and friends.

"John," Jeanne said, "I think working at the UN would be a wonderful experience for you. As for me, I imagine living in New York City would be quite exciting!"

"Then let's make the move!" John smiled.

John Humphrey and Eleanor Roosevelt at the UN, about 1947.

Returning the call from Monsieur Laugier, John spoke excitedly, "You're right, Henri. *Ce sera une grande aventure!*" [It will be a great adventure!]

A few weeks later, John and Jeanne moved to New York City, and John began his work at the UN. One of the first persons John met at the UN was Eleanor Roosevelt, chairperson of the Human Rights Commission. Eleanor was the widow of former United States President, Franklin D. Roosevelt.

"John," Eleanor requested. "I'd like you to write a list of rules which will describe how people around the world should be treated."

"I will do my best, Mrs. Roosevelt," John replied, with confidence.

"We'll call it ... a Human Rights Declaration!" Eleanor said triumphantly.

John left the UN headquarters that afternoon, feeling a little overwhelmed by Mrs. Roosevelt's request.

As he walked home, John admitted, "It's a tremendous task, but one that may create one of the greatest moments in history when it is finally completed, approved and ratified by the nations of the world!"

"How will I write this declaration? Where will I start?" John wondered, as he passed a group of children playing in a park. Suddenly, childhood memories began dancing in his head.

John's a one-armed Doukhobor... Leave my brother alone... That's a licking you won't forget in a hurry... There goes Fatty... Disobedience will not be tolerated, Humphrey... John, you will need to discover, in your own way, how to do with one hand all the things that other people can do with two...

"I must start writing," John determined, when he reached his apartment. "I'll write a set of rules so that the rights of everyone, even the weak, will be respected."

John tapped his pencil on the desk and chewed on the end of his pipe.

"If everyone is entitled to the same basic rights and freedoms, whether they are male or female, old or young, rich or poor, light-skinned or dark-skinned, one-handed or two, then maybe the world will be a better place in which to live!"

For months John wrote and revised forty-eight rules, called 'articles'. A man named René Cassin from France and others took the draft, made more revisions, and shortened the number of articles to thirty.

When John read the final copy, he confided in his wife, "I'm glad *The Declaration* has been completed. But I'm disappointed that the articles on minority groups were deleted. Minorities like First Nations People and Japanese Canadians need to feel included and protected."

On December 10, 1948, John breathed a sigh of relief when the UN General Assembly – meeting in Paris, France – adopted the *Universal Declaration of Human Rights*.

> **IN 1950,
> THE UN NAMED DECEMBER 10TH,
> INTERNATIONAL
> HUMAN RIGHTS DAY.**

The *Magna Carta,* or Great Charter, was a document created by English Barons (rich landowners) and signed by King John of England in 1215. The purpose of the charter was to grant rights and liberties to English subjects, and to limit the power of the king. The *Magna Carta* was one of the most important documents of Medieval England.

Mrs. Roosevelt holding the "*Magna Carta* of all mankind".

Mrs. Roosevelt was delighted. "This *Universal Declaration of Human Rights* may well become the International *Magna Carta* of all mankind [people] everywhere!" she exclaimed.

Nearly two years before *The Declaration* was adopted, Eleanor Roosevelt had spoken at the Montreal Forum before an audience of over 8,000 people. At the event, Mrs. Roosevelt told her audience that she was particularly indebted to Canada for John Humphrey, Director of the Human Rights Division at the UN.

The Montreal Star [February 26, 1947] reported part of Mrs. Roosevelt's speech: "I have been grateful to John Humphrey every day of our session because he has provided so much background material and has done such a very excellent job."

John Humphrey would become a hero. But for decades, most people wouldn't know who John was or what he had written. And John wasn't the kind of person to brag.

Thanks to John Humphrey sharing his ideas, *The Declaration* would provide a new world vision; that human rights are for everyone – every individual girl, boy, man, and woman, all around the world.

John knew that *The Declaration* was only a first step to making equal rights come true for all people. There was still a lot of work to do.

Chapter 23

Protecting the Bullied

John Humphrey visits a children's camp near Ulan Bator, Mongolia, 1965.

John continued working at the UN until 1966. During this very demanding time in his life, John still kept in touch with his family back in New Brunswick. Each year John would send his aunts and uncles a Christmas card, and he often visited them during his summer vacation.

John's relatives marvelled at his important position at the UN.

"I'm amazed at how many different countries John has been to!" Uncle Percy remarked, as he opened John's Christmas card.

His son Jack agreed, "When I saw John last summer, he told me about all the negotiations he's been doing. It's incredible how much that boy travels!"

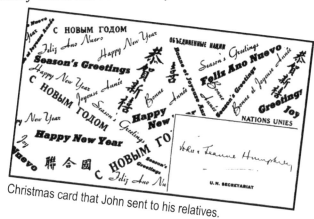

Christmas card that John sent to his relatives.

For years, John travelled all over the world, representing the UN at international conventions, or meetings. John was an excellent negotiator – very skilled in communicating with others and passionately persistent about human rights. He was definitely not a quitter.

John helped political leaders to write laws which

Evening Times-Globe

Saint John, N.B.   March 13, 1959

UNITED NATIONS, N.Y. (Canadian Press)

Sitting in his office high in the UN skyscraper, Humphrey took a deep breath and added: "You can say my job is interesting – fascinating, in fact – frustrating."

It includes much travel – Humphrey was around the world last year – and supervision here [at the UN] of 30 professional officers and 20 general staff members from some twenty countries.

respected the human rights and freedoms of their countries' citizens. The *Universal Declaration of Human Rights* served as an indispensable guide in writing these laws.

On one occasion in the 1950s, following a three-day convention in Geneva, John arrived at the Swiss airport just in time to catch his flight to New York City. He was looking forward to going home.

"I feel tired, but satisfied with the progress we made," John reflected to himself optimistically, as he settled in his seat on the plane. "I had to work hard at the meetings, convincing those leaders to consider the importance of individual human rights."

John arrived at the airport, just in time to catch his flight home to New York City.

John Humphrey (right), at a convention on the Status of Refugees, in Geneva, 1951.

Seated in the large airplane beside him was a young man named Ken, who worked for the World Health Organization in Geneva. Ken and John started chatting.

"These last three days have been a challenge," John admitted to Ken. "But I've been facing challenges ever since I was a child! I should be used to it by now!"

"A child?" Ken questioned.

"Yes, I was bullied a lot because of my missing arm," John explained, as he pointed to his empty left sleeve. "I can't begin to count the number of fights I was in."

"And now you're a negotiator for peace," Ken smiled.

"It's hard to believe," John nodded, "that I used to try solving problems by fighting!"

"What made you change?" Ken inquired.

John shifted in his seat as he chuckled, "I think I started to change when I realized I was losing nearly every fight!"

Ken laughed.

"Maybe it's good I only had one arm, and one fist," John continued. "Losing one fight after another made me realize that I needed to find a better way to beat the bullies!"

After the flight attendant brought them their supper meal, Ken asked, "How did kids bully you?"

"They teased me," John said.

As an adult, John learned more about the Doukhobors – beyond the teasing he'd received as a child. He discovered that as pacifists, the Doukhobors had refused to serve in the Russian army and left Russia in order to avoid persecution. Over 7000 Doukhobors emigrated from Russia to Canada in 1899, six years before John was born.

Article 14 in *The Declaration* was written for people like the Doukhobors.

Everyone has the right to seek and to enjoy in other countries asylum from persecution (a safe place to live).

"They called me a one-armed Doukhobor."

"Ah, I bet you hated that," remarked Ken.

"Yes, I certainly did," John nodded. "It would send me into a fury!"

"As a child, it's hard to handle teasing," Ken commented knowingly.

"Yes. Sometimes I would feel so helpless to stop them, that I'd be afraid to go to school," John admitted. "I remember feeling so embarrassed that I just wanted to hide somewhere..."

"Did your parents ever know you were being bullied?" Ken asked.

"My father died when I was a baby. My mother was wonderful but she died when I was eleven. I found it especially hard after that."

"What incredible resilience!" Ken declared. "Look at the way you've moved forward in your life after being so badly bullied as a child!"

"But because of all the times I was bullied," John explained, "I can understand how it feels for others who are bullied. And now I'm able to help stop those who think that hurting others is okay."

"Hmmm. I can see that you are well-suited to your job," Ken commented warmly.

"Yes," John reflected. "I feel very strongly about human rights."

The McGill Reporter

Montreal, Quebec   March 23, 1995

...In an interview in the Toronto Star in 1988, John Humphrey recalled the hard lessons learned early.

"It was pretty tough as a youngster having only one arm. Other kids used to taunt me...and I'd lose my cool and get into fights. It's tough for a youngster who is incapacitated. Children can be cruel. But I survived the fights. And those early experiences taught me about injustice and the need for human rights."...

"You're an inspiration," Ken remarked. "There's no finer contribution you could make than devoting your life to protecting people all around the world!"

John smiled and tipped his chair back. Before long, he had nodded off. His napping was soon interrupted, however, by the irritated voice of a belligerent man, seated across the aisle from him. The man was annoyed with his wife.

John and Jeanne in their New York apartment.

"Your jobs are cooking, cleaning, and the children. I do the important stuff, because I'm the boss of this family!"

The wife remained silent.

John cringed and muttered to Ken, "And some men bully their wives! Not to mention belittle the work that they do – the very important work of raising children! Laws must change," John insisted, "so that women have equal rights and are valued for the work they do at home!"

Finally their plane landed at the Idlewild Airport in New York City. John and Ken shook hands as they said good-bye.

John hurried to pick up his luggage; he was anxious to get home and see Jeanne. John had missed his wife and was looking forward to their weekly walk in Central Park. It would be good to be home.

John was due to retire in 1965 because the UN required their employees to stop work at age sixty. Since John had work to complete, he was allowed to stay an extra year.

Friday, April 29, 1966

CALLS IT A DAY
UNITED NATIONS

Canadian-born Dr. John P. Humphrey retires today after 20 years as Director of the United Nations Division of Human Rights. He will return to an academic career at McGill University. But, said Humphrey, often referred to as Mr. Human Rights at the UN, he is not retiring from work in the field of human rights. He has been elected to membership on the sub-commission on prevention of discrimination and protection of minorities – a subsidiary group of the Human Rights Commission. The tall and blue-eyed native of Hampton, N.B., said he will attend meetings of the sub-commission in January as one of its 18 experts.

139

One evening at supper, John said, "In another month Jeanne, I'll have my UN work completed. How quickly the last twenty years have gone!"

With a wealth of experience and a special talent for teaching, John returned to McGill, to a job he loved. Around the university, you could hear law students talking eagerly.

Evening Times-Globe

Saint John, N.B.   March 16, 1995

… [Dr. Margaret Kunstler] made specific mention of John's devotion to teaching. "His greatest joy was to help young students and to lead them along good paths of understanding. He used to receive letters from them [his former students] recalling his unusual kindness…"

"Be sure and take Professor Humphrey's course in International Law," one student remarked. "He's a hard marker but he's so passionate about what he's teaching!"

"It's the best law course I've ever taken," another student agreed.

John was glad to be back at the university. He enjoyed living in Montreal, with the opportunity to experience both English and French cultures. But there was sadness ahead.

One day, Jeanne noticed something was wrong with her muscles.

"My handwriting seems to be getting smaller," Jeanne remarked to John, "and my left arm is shaking. I … I can't seem to stop it."

Jeanne had Parkinson's disease and it got progressively worse. It became difficult for her to get around and she was slower at doing everyday tasks. Sadly, over time, Jeanne lost more and more mobility and had to stop travelling. Used to having Jeanne travel with him, John hated leaving her behind.

"Jeanne, I'll be gone a week," John would say to her. "I've arranged for your dinners to be brought in. I wish you could come with me!"

For many years Jeanne struggled with her illness. Whenever he was home, John did whatever he could do to make life easier for her.

In 1980, the year following John and Jeanne's fiftieth wedding anniversary, Jeanne died. John was terribly sad to lose his wife.

Chapter 24

Romance at 76

John and his second wife, Margaret Kunstler.

John was invited to a dinner party in Montreal (a year after Jeanne's death), where he met Margaret Kunstler, a widowed medical doctor. John and Margaret seemed to enjoy each other's company, and spent most of the evening talking together.

As John took a taxi home to his apartment, he wondered, "Is it a coincidence that both Margaret and I were there tonight... or was it planned?"

At seventy-six, John didn't want to waste any time. He proposed to Margaret a few days following the dinner party and Margaret accepted. John was delighted! Three weeks later they were married.

One evening at home, John remarked to his new wife, "Margaret, did you know that dinner party where we met was a set-up?"

Margaret nodded, "Our friends planned it so we'd meet."

"I guess they were right," John laughed. "We are a good match!"

John, not used to large family gatherings, was overwhelmed at first by the size of Margaret's family. He soon learned to enjoy his new extended family which included Margaret's two adult daughters, Dorothy and Moni, and their families.

John and Margaret enjoyed fourteen years together. They went on many trips to far-away countries, while John continued his work promoting human rights.

Although John was always devoted to his work, he also enjoyed taking time to relax and have fun. For nearly thirty years, he spent summer holidays at his beloved cottage at Brackley Beach on Prince Edward Island. In later years, he taught a summer-school course on Human Rights at the University of Prince Edward Island.

John, relaxing at the cottage.

Whether it was at McGill with his university students, or at UPEI with school teachers, John never missed an opportunity to teach others about the importance of individual human rights. John's students loved having him as a teacher. But they didn't know their beloved law professor had written the draft copy of the *Universal Declaration of Human Rights*!

Chapter 25

International Hero

Law Librarian John Hobbins and John Humphrey.

"**I** can't believe it!" Mr. Hobbins marvelled as he pulled hand-written pages from a filing cabinet.

John Hobbins, Law Librarian at McGill University, made a very important discovery, forty years after the *Universal Declaration of Human Rights* had been adopted by the UN.

"This is a complete draft of *The Declaration*, in Professor Humphrey's handwriting! I never knew that Professor Humphrey drafted the *Universal Declaration of Human Rights*! Does anyone else know? This is amazing!"

No one at McGill knew. In fact, only John's immediate family and a few close friends were aware that John had drafted *The Declaration*.

The McGill Reporter, November 2, 1988.

"People should know about the outstanding contribution John Humphrey has made to the world!" Mr. Hobbins said, with determination.

Others agreed that everyone must learn the truth. Very quickly, Mr. Hobbins spread the word.

On December 8, 1988, John was flown to the UN Headquarters in New York City. At the General Assembly, John was presented with the United Nations' Human Rights Award.

John Humphrey, the boy who was bullied, had become an international hero! Pleased by the recognition, but embarrassed by all the attention, 83-year-old John simply nodded and said,

"I was just doing my job."

The Telegraph Journal

Saint John, N.B.   Friday, December 9, 1988

Hampton native honoured by UN for role in forging human rights document

UNITED NATIONS, N.Y. (Canadian Press) The General Assembly honored Canadian John Humphrey on Thursday for his role in forging the Universal Declaration of Human Rights, a document praised for showing the world the "path to human dignity." …

Walking slowly, but sounding hardy, Humphrey joined others on the platform of the Assembly Hall to receive a brass and wooden plaque carved with a flame, symbolizing human rights.

"It turns out the achievement of 1948 was much greater than anybody would have dared to imagine at the time," he said later in an interview.

John Humphrey, international hero.

John Humphrey,
the boy who was bullied.

Epilogue

John worked for human rights his whole life. He never missed an opportunity to teach his students –

"There is a fundamental connection between human rights and peace. We will have peace on earth when everyone's rights are respected."

The McGill Reporter, November 23, 1988.

John and Margaret enjoyed entertaining, both at their summer cottage in Prince Edward Island and at their home in Montreal. John was always delighted to participate in lively and challenging conversations. Over the years, they entertained many distinguished guests, including: ambassadors to the UN (such as Gérard Pelletier, also a former federal cabinet minister), professionals from Africa (such as Professor Agnes Ndabakwaje from the University of Bujumbura in Burundi), representatives on the European Court of Justice (such as Canadian Judge Ronald Macdonald), and even former Prime Minister Pierre Elliott Trudeau.

In his senior years, John was often called on to speak at national and international conferences, sharing his knowledge of Human Rights.

John, speaking at an International Jurists conference, 1985.

The United Nations had tremendous respect for John's expertise as a peace negotiator. In the summer of 1994, the UN flew 89-year-old John to the Middle East, to facilitate peace negotiations between Israel and Palestine. At that point, the conflict between these two nations had been going on for nearly fifty years.

On their return flight to Canada, John sadly admitted to Margaret, "I tried my best to help the Palestinian and Israeli people. But they wouldn't even talk to each other."

John felt discouraged that his efforts for peace in the Middle East had not seemed to help make a difference. Realizing that he did not have the same energy he once had, John felt sad that he might not be able to carry on this work much longer. His greatest wish was that others would carry on his mission, with a commitment to work for the rights of all people around the world.

One spring evening in 1995, John's McGill University friends and colleagues held a retirement party in his honour. They wanted John to know how much they appreciated him and how much they had learned from him. John was very touched by this celebration.

That evening, in his speech to the assembled guests, John concluded by saying, "*A bas la collectivité* "; meaning – individual rights are more important than collective or group rights. These were John's last public words.

That night after the party, John had a heart attack. A week later, seven weeks short of his 90th birthday, John died.

John's family and friends felt sad about their loss. At the same time, they were pleased to have been a part of John's life – a life full of adventure and accomplishments.

John's tombstone, located in Hampton Rural Cemetery.

Hampton-born professor drafted UN's blueprint for human rights

The Hampton-born man who wrote the first draft of the United Nations' *Universal Declaration of Human Rights* died peacefully in Montreal on Tuesday morning…

The man who grew up to be a mover and shaker in the early years of the United Nations spent his own early years in Hampton…

Hampton resident Leah MacGowan, now 90 years old, still remembers him as a "handsome little guy" with rare pluck. "He had a lot of uphill things he had to do in life, but he had that spirit of conquering and coming out on top that coloured his life," Mrs. MacGowan said yesterday.

A colleague, Professor Irwin Cotler of the McGill University School of Law, said Professor Humphrey was "that rare find in the halls of academe –someone who not only teaches international law, but embodies it." Prof. Cotler said that he and all professors of international law "are really forever students of this man and of his inspiration and handiwork."

Prof. Humphrey's curriculum vitae is extraordinary – nearly three pages of honour upon honour...

Besides numerous articles on international politics and legal subjects, Prof. Humphrey wrote several books…

His step-grandson, Walter Malone, a photographer in Saint John, said that Prof. Humphrey, for all his brushes with great figures, never lost the common touch. "He was a quiet man – you'd never guess he had dealt with kings and queens."

John's Accomplishments

➤ As a child, John was able to rise above three tragedies – the death of his father, the loss of his left arm, and the death of his mother.

➤ In 1920, at age fifteen, John succeeded in passing the Provincial High School Exams, for entrance to university.

➤ In 1925, John earned a Bachelor of Commerce degree from McGill University.

➤ In 1927, John earned a Bachelor of Arts degree from McGill.

➤ In 1929, John earned a Bachelor of Civil Law degree from McGill.

➤ In 1945, John earned a Ph.D. degree in Political Science from McGill.

➤ In 1945, at age forty, John was appointed Dean of the Faculty of Law, at McGill.

PhD. Graduates: John, back row, 2nd from left.

➤ In 1946, John was appointed the first Director of the Human Rights Division of the UN Secretariat.

First meeting of the UN Human Rights Commission at Lake Success, New York, 1947.
Front, l-r: Eleanor Roosevelt, John Humphrey, Charles Malik and others.

> In 1947, John wrote the draft copy of the UN *Universal Declaration of Human Rights.*

One page of the draft copy of *The Declaration*, in John Humphrey's handwriting.

> From 1946 to 1966, during his twenty years at the UN, John met with many world leaders and negotiated at 67 conventions. These meetings resulted in human-rights laws being passed in countries that never before had considered individual rights.

12 Nations sign Refugee Convention, Geneva, Switzerland, July, 1951. Front row, 2nd from left, is John Humphrey, Negotiator for the UN.

John and Castel Borja (Philippines) at a meeting of the Human Rights Commission, 1964.

John with Ethiopian Emperor Haile Selassie, 1960.

John greeting Mother Teresa, about 1990.

➢ From 1946 until his death, John's influence on human rights issues was felt around the world – particularly in the areas of Freedom of the Press, Status of Women, and Racial Discrimination.

John (front row) speaks at a conference on *The Participation of Women in Public Life*, in Addis Ababa, Ethiopia, 1960.

- As a member of an International Commission of Inquiry, John travelled to the Philippines to investigate human rights violations on one occasion, and on another, he represented Korean women forced into captivity in Japan.

- In 1967, John was the Founding President of the Canadian Human Rights Foundation.

- In 1973, John co-founded Amnesty International Canada.

- In 1974, John became an Officer of the Order of Canada, recognized for his world-wide efforts in human rights.

Amnesty International Group, Hampton, N.B.

- In 1977, John (age 72), and Ruth (age 78), both received honorary doctorate degrees from Mount Allison University. Over the years, John received thirteen honorary doctorates from universities around the world.

l-r, Ruth Humphrey, Hon. Romeo LeBlanc, Dr. John Humphrey, President Dr. W.S.H. Crawford, Mount Allison University.

- In 1985, John received the National Order of Quebec.

- In 1988, at 83 years of age, John received the prestigious United Nations' Human Rights Award.

- In 1992, the International Centre for Human Rights and Democratic Development established the Rights and Democracy's *John Humphrey Award*, ($30,000) which is presented each year in honour of John – recognizing the exceptional contribution of an organization or individual in the field of human rights.

[On March 14, 1995, John Humphrey died. Following his death, John's legacy continued to be honoured.]

- In 1998, many special events took place to celebrate the 50th anniversary of the adoption of the *Universal Declaration of Human Rights*.

- In June, 1998, the National Arts Centre in Ottawa honoured John with an exhibit entitled, *Citizen of the World*. At the time of the opening, exhibition curator, Gerry Grace, said, "This exhibition is more than important documents; it is a celebration of a great Canadian. It is too often the case that Canadians do not know their heroes. I am pleased the National Arts Centre is providing Canadians with a chance to learn about this remarkable person whose ideas and writings changed the world."

THE KINGS COUNTY RECORD

SUSSEX, KINGS COUNTY, N.B.   JULY 21, 1998

From left to right: Noel Kinsella (AHRC director), UN Secretary-General Javier Perez de Cuellar, and Dr. John Peters Humphrey.

Humphrey display at arts centre, face to appear on postage stamp

- In July, 1998, Maclean's Magazine named John Humphrey one of the most important Canadians in history. *Few Canadians have had such impact on modern history,* Maclean's stated.

- In September 1998, Nelson Mandela, former President of South Africa, unveiled a memorial bronze plaque in Ottawa, honouring John. Mandela referred to John Humphrey as "the father of the modern human rights system".

- In October, 1998, Canada Post issued a stamp in John's memory. The stamp was designed by Jim Hudson of Moncton, N.B.

- In 2000, the John Humphrey Centre for Peace and Human Rights opened in Edmonton, Alberta. Their website is www.jhcentre.org

- In 2000, the Hampton John Peters Humphrey Foundation was formed. Its mission is to provide an ongoing tribute to John, by educating others about his life and accomplishments, and educating people of all ages about human-rights issues.

- In 2008, under the leadership of the Hampton John Peters Humphrey Foundation, a human rights sculpture, called *Credo,* was erected. Created by Hooper Studios, *Credo* is located in the center of Hampton, on the Courthouse lawn. It is the Foundation's way of celebrating John's long-lasting contribution to world-wide human rights, and ensuring that their home-town boy is no longer an unsung hero. Website: humphreyhampton.org

Credo sculpture, Hampton, N.B.

Bibliography

Books:

Hampton Women's Institute, *The Tweedsmuir Village History of Hampton.* Edited by Mabel (Scovil) Humphrey and Helen Scovil, Hampton, NB,1953.

Hobbins, A.J., Editor, *On The Edge of Greatness, The Diaries of John Humphrey, First Director of the United Nations, Division of Human Rights. Volume 1, 1948-1949,* McGill University Libraries.

Humphrey, J.P., (c. 1990). *Life is an adventure.* Unpublished manuscript. McGill University Archives, MG4127, Container 8, File 133, "Life is an adventure."

Keirstead, David G., *Hampton Consolidated School, A Story Worth Telling.* Kings County Historical and Archival Society, Hampton,NB, 2007.

Keirstead, David G., *Reflections: The Story of Hampton, N.B.* Kings County Historical and Archival Society, Hampton, NB, 1983.

Kielburger, Craig, *Free The Children.* Me to We Books, Toronto, ON, 2007.

Nicholson, G.W.L., *Official History of the Canadian Army in the First World War: Canadian Expeditionary Force 1914-1919.* 1962. Queens Printer and Controller of Stationery, Ottawa, Canada

The HHS Memoria Military Heritage Project, Hampton High School. *Hampton Remembers.* Hampton, NB, 2008.

The World Book Encyclopedia, Volume 21. *World War I and World War II.* World Book, Inc. Chicago, Illinois, 1990.

Internet Sites:

http://en.wikipedia.org/wiki/Samuel_Leonard_Tilley
http://www.archives.mcgill.ca/public/exhibits/humphrey/Home/HRposter.html
http://www.histori.ca/minutes/minute.do?id=10219
http://www.histori.ca/minutes/minute.do?id=13579
http://wn.com/John_Peters_Humphrey
www.un.org/cyberschoolbus/humanrights/resources/plain.asp

Journal and Magazine Articles, Address, Documentary, and Correspondence:

Maclean's Magazine, Toronto, ON, July 1, 1998. *The 100 Most Important Canadians in History.*

McGill Journal of Education, McGill University, Montreal, QC. *Life at RCS.* John Humphrey's letters to his sister Ruth, 1919.

National Arts Centre News, Ottawa, ON, June 30, 1998. [John Humphrey]*Citizen of the World.*

Punch Magazine, London, England, December, 1915. *In Flanders Fields* by John McCrae.

The Vancouver Observer, Vancouver, BC, December 8, 2010. Veniez, Daniel D. *The Lessons of John Humphrey.*

Address to the Canadian Association of Statutory Human Rights Agencies Conference, Fredericton, NB, June 16, 2006. Kinsella, Noel. *Tribute to John Peters Humphrey.*

Vision TV, Toronto, ON, December 10, 1992. *By His Hand,* documentary profile of John Peters Humphrey.

Correspondence from Ralph March, Vancouver, BC, addressed to Harold Wright, Saint John, NB, 1985. re growing up in Hampton.

Newspaper Articles:

Evening Times-Globe, Saint John, NB, Mar. 13, 1959; Mar. 16, 1995; July 3, 1998; Dec.10, 1998.

Kings County Record, Sussex, NB, June 8, 1906; March 11, 1911; June 23, 1916; Sept. 22, 1916; March 28, 1995; July 21, 1998.

Montreal Star, Montreal, QC, Feb. 26, 1947

The McGill Reporter. McGill University, Montreal, QC, Nov. 2, Nov. 23, 1988; March 23, 1995.

The Telegraph Journal, Saint John, NB, Dec. 9, 1988; March 16, 1995; Dec. 10, 1998

Toronto Sun, Toronto, ON, April 19, 1995.

Photo Credits

The photos in this book are used with permission and through the courtesy of: *(t=top, b=bottom, l=left, r=right, c=centre)*

Ethiopian Embassy, Ottawa, ON. pp.150-cl, KMBT250, No. 669; 150-b, KMBT250, No.616.

Heritage Resources Saint John, Saint John, NB. pp.20-t; 43; 59; 67; 78; 85; 112-t; 112-b; 136.

Humphrey Family Scrapbooks. pp..18-b; 19-c; 22-t; 22-bl; 25; 37; 45; 50-b; 76; 86-b; 94-tr; 120; 121; 126; 127-t; 127-b; 131; 132; 135-b; 139; 144-br; 145; 152-b; 153-c.

International Centre for Human Rights and Democratic Development, Montreal, QC. p.152-t, John Humphrey Freedom Award poster.

John Fisher Museum, Kingston, NB. pp.24-t; 54; 58-t; 92 (detail).

Kings County Historical and Archival Society, Hampton, NB. pp.8; 13-14; 15-b; 16; 17-tl; 17-c; 17-b; 18-t; 23-t (detail); 29; 32; 33(detail); 38-41; 49; 58-b (detail); 68-t; 69; 73-75; 91-t; 97; 105-t; 106.

Library and Archives Canada, Toronto, ON. p.130-b, PA-168131.

Masonic Lodge, Hampton, NB. pp.17-tr; 19-tl; 20-bl; 21-t.

McCord Museum, Montreal, QC. pp.61-b, 15809; 63-b, 105910.2; 124, 15468.

McGill University Archives, Montreal, QC. pp.19-tr, Climo/McGill Archives, 2002-0086.04.001; 21-c, 2002-0086.04.004.1; 96, 2002-0086.04.003; 108; 129-t, 2002-0086.04; 129-b; 143-t, Jack Goldsmith/photographer, 2002-0086.04.194; 143-b; 145-t; 148-c, 0000-1040.02.

Mount Allison University Archives, Sackville, NB. pp.122, unaccessioned; 123, 2008.25/9; 151-b.

New Brunswick Museum, Saint John, NB. pp.30, 1988.64.13; 56, 5335-P49; 64, X16706.231; 86-t,16961; 94-b, 12796.

Photographs from individuals, as noted in Acknowledgements.

Photographer unknown. p.144-bl, Extensive research revealed: Paris, 1984.

Provincial Archives of New Brunswick, Fredericton, NB. pp.46, George Taylor fonds: P5-198; 57, Les Religieuses Hospitalières de Saint-Joseph, P24-12; 60, Thomas Duncan collection: P111-40; 68-b, Les Religieuses Hospitalières de Saint-Joseph, P24-18; 84, Nashwaak Family Bicentennial Association collection: P145-36; 103, Assorted Photo Acquisitions #6: P194-213; 115, Fonds du père Jean-Marie Courtois, Eudistes: P38-101; 116, Fonds du père Jean–Marie Courtois, Eudistes: P38-100A.

Rothesay Netherwood School Archives, Rothesay, NB. pp.102; 105-b(detail); 111; 113.

Royal Canadian Legion, Branch #28, Hampton, NB. p.87.

The 8th Hussars Regimental Museum, Sussex, NB. p.90.

The John C. Winston Co., 1919, Toronto, ON. p.88.

United Nations Archives, New York City, NY, USA. pp.9, 63484, 126485; 94-tl, 99367; 130-t, 170728 (detail); 134, 1292; 137, 170910; 148-b, 118242; 150-tl, 170912; 150-tr, 112838; 158-t, 123898.

Université Laval, Quebec City, QC. Marc Robitaille/Photographer (photographer granted permission). p.150-cr.

Wilson Studio Collection, Hampton, NB. pp.12; 15-t; 47-t (detail).

Children Learn About Human Rights

John Humphrey's wish was that future generations, especially those living in countries like Canada, where human rights are often taken for granted – accept responsibility for continuing the quest for human rights... for all individuals, all around the world.

John felt very strongly that children needed to learn about human rights so that they could carry on the message.

Children of the UN International Nursery School look at a poster of *The Declaration.* New York, 1950.

Children at Hampton Elementary School perform in the musical, "Peace Cranes", a play about Human Rights and the life of John Peters Humphrey; Hampton, N.B., 2000.

Guide for Teachers

Students may enjoy acting out the six skits [p.161-167] illustrating some of the articles in the *Universal Declaration of Human Rights.* They may also want to create their own drama. The skits can be used to generate discussion on a variety of human-rights issues (of a local or global nature).

Here are some questions that students may want to reflect on:

1. Many children have suffered from tragedies and bullying. In light of this, what makes John's situation similar, or different?
   - How did John's adventurous, determined personality play a role?
   - How did John's resilience lead him to success?
   - Discuss how John's childhood – the tragedies, the bullying, and the love from his family – may have influenced him in later years.

2. Consider the major advancements which have occurred in medicine since the early 1900s. If John's burning accident had occurred today, his arm would likely have been saved. If John had not lost his arm, how might his life have been different?

3. How, when, and by whom, is empathy shown toward John? How does John show empathy toward others?

4. What role is the UN currently playing with respect to human-rights issues throughout the world?

5. What part can students and teachers play in continuing John Humphrey's legacy, by improving the human rights of the individual? Research the human-rights work that activists, such as Craig Kielburger, have initiated. Website: www.freethechildren.com What other organizations are there in Canada that work to improve human rights, both locally and globally?

Please note: Teachers have permission to photocopy the skits, for use in the classroom.

The Declaration articles listed below (in plain language) are illustrated in the skits:

Article 1 – (articulated by the two-line rap, a part of each skit)
When people are born, they are free and each should be treated in the same way. They have reason and conscience and should act towards one another in a friendly manner.

Article 2 – (Skits 1, 2, and 3)
Everyone can claim the following rights, despite – a different sex, a different skin colour, speaking a different language, thinking different things, believing in another religion, owning more or less, being born in another social group, coming from another country.

Article 4 (Skit 6)
Nobody has the right to treat you as his or her slave and you should not make anyone your slave.

Article 12 (Skit 4)
You have the right to ask to be protected if someone tries to harm your good name, enter your house, open your letters, read your diary, or bother you or your family without a good reason.

Article 19 (Skit 5)
You have the right to think what you want, to say what you like, and nobody should forbid you from doing so. You should be able to share your ideas also – with people from any other country.

Article 1

(original text)

All human beings are born free and equal, in dignity and rights...

Children beside sculpture of John Humphrey, in Hampton, N.B.

| Human Rights for everyone | Not just a chosen few | Each person is important | Including me and you! |

Skit 1 – Rights, Regardless of Race or Colour

Everyone is entitled to all the rights and freedoms..., without distinction of any kind, such as race or colour.
PARTS: (7) – 4 light-skinned people, Owen, Greg, Steven, Jack; 1 dark-skinned person, Kaywan; and 2 Human Rights Defenders (HRDs).

SCENE: A group of children stand and chat. Owen tosses a soccer ball.

OWEN – Let's play soccer.

JACK – Count me in.

KAYWAN – Me, too.

OWEN – Hey, you're not on our team, Loser. *(looks at the other light-skinned boys for support)*

GREG – *(laughs)* Yeah, you might be a terrorist.

KAYWAN *(hesitates)* – I wasn't born here, but I live here now.

STEVEN – Oh, let the loser play!

HRD #1 and #2 – *(run into the scene, shouting)* FREEZE! *(Group freezes.)*
    (HRDs start rapping) **Human Rights for everyone, not just a chosen few.
                Each person is important, including me and you!**

HRD #2 – Calling people names really hurts. Sometimes it's worse than broken bones. And the hurt lasts longer!

HRD #1 – It's important to speak up and defend others who are being called names. UNFREEZE! *(HRDs freeze.)*

JACK – *(speaks to Greg)* Hey, buddy, leave him alone. He's okay. He's cool.

GREG – Alright, I'm sorry.

OWEN – Okay, you can join us. Let's play soccer.

    [Boys exit. HRDs cheer, high five, and exit.]

| Human Rights for everyone | Not just a chosen few | Each person is important | Including me and you! |

Skit 2 — Rights, Regardless of Gender

Everyone is entitled to all the rights and freedoms..., without distinction of any kind, such as gender (male or female).

PARTS: (7) – Emma, Matt, Nick, Joe, Sophie and 2 Human Rights Defenders (HRDs).

SCENE: Some boys work on building a camp. As Emma walks over, the boys stop hammering.

EMMA – Hi guys. Can I help?

MATT – Are you serious? We're building a camp. We don't want **girls** here!

EMMA – (*protests*) But, I'm good at hammering!

NICK – (*laughs*) Oh yeah? Show us. (*Emma hammers in a nail.*)

MATT – Not bad... but still, no girls allowed!

JOE – Sorry, boys only!

HRD #1 and #2 – (*run into the scene, shouting*) FREEZE! (*Group freezes.*)
   (*HRDs start rapping.*) **Human Rights for everyone, not just a chosen few.**
                  Each person is important, including me and you!

HRD #1 – Both girls and boys should be treated fairly.

HRD #2 – Both boys and girls should have equal rights. UNFREEZE!
   (*HRDs freeze.*)

JOE – Emma, maybe you **could** help us.

NICK – Yeah, I guess. Bring a friend, too, if you want.
   (*Emma runs over to Sophie and tugs her toward the camp construction. The girls start hammering beside the boys.*)

SOPHIE – (*smiles at Emma*) Don't worry, they'll get used to us!

MATT – Let's take a break and have some ice cream.

EMMA – Good idea!

   (*Boys and girls exit together. HRDs cheer, high five, and exit.*)

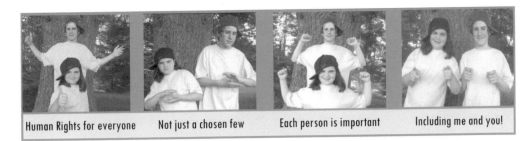

Human Rights for everyone   Not just a chosen few   Each person is important   Including me and you!

SKIT 3 — RIGHTS, REGARDLESS OF STATUS

Everyone is entitled to all the rights and freedoms..., without distinction of any kind, such as (social) status.

PARTS: (6) – Laura, Grace, Rayanne, Bonnie and 2 Human Rights Defenders (HRDs).
SCENE: Three girls sit on a bench and talk about their summer vacations. A girl named Bonnie sits at the other end of the bench by herself.

LAURA – I just got back from
   Prince Edward Island. We rented a cottage for two weeks!
GRACE – My family went camping at Fundy National Park.
RAYANNE – I went to Quebec for a gymnastics camp. It was totally awesome!
GRACE – (*leans forward*) Hey, Bonnie, where did you go?
BONNIE – (*turns and shrugs her shoulders*) I stayed here.
LAURA – (*taunts*) Why didn't you go away, Bonnie?
BONNIE – Well, my mom had to work.
RAYANNE – (*whispers loudly*) Look what Bonnie's wearing! It looks like it
   belongs to her grandmother! (*Bonnie buries her head in her hands and the
   other girls laugh.*)
HRD #1 and #2 – (*run into the scene, shouting*) FREEZE! (*Group freezes.*)
   (*HRDs start rapping.*) **Human Rights for everyone, not just a chosen few.**
           Each person is important, including me and you!
HRD #1 – Everyone has the right to be treated politely – even if they are
   poor or not popular.
HRD #2 – Yeah, being nice is cool. UNFREEZE! (*HRDs freeze.*)
LAURA – Bonnie – Grace and Rayanne are coming over to my house. Do you
   want to come?
BONNIE – You're asking me to come to your house?
LAURA – Yes, please come.
BONNIE – Sure, I'd love to! And thanks for asking.
GRACE – Let's go! (*Girls exit together. HRDs cheer, high five, and exit.*)

| Human Rights for everyone | Not just a chosen few | Each person is important | Including me and you! |

Skit 4 — The Right to Privacy

No one shall be subjected to interference with his or her privacy.

PARTS: (6) – Amelia, Katie, Maria, Ryan and 2 Human Rights Defenders (HRDs).
SCENE: Sitting alone, Amelia writes in her diary. As she writes, she speaks aloud.

AMELIA – Dear Diary, this was an awful day at school. It's been the most embarrassing day of my life. In math class, Mrs. Wilson asked me… (*Maria runs past Amelia, grabs her diary and passes it to Katie.*)

KATIE – Listen to this, Maria. (*Teasingly, she reads from the diary*) "Mrs. Wilson asked me a question and when I didn't know the answer, she glared at me. I was scared…" What a sissy! (*passes diary to Maria*)

MARIA - Mrs. Wilson! She's not scary!

HRD #1 and #2 – (*run into the scene, shouting*) FREEZE! (*Group freezes.*)

(*HRDs start rapping.*) **Human Rights for everyone, not just a chosen few. Each person is important, including me and you!**

HRD #1 – Everyone has a right to their own private thoughts.

HRD #2 – Yes, privacy is important! UNFREEZE! (*HRDs freeze.*)

MARIA – (*hands diary back to Amelia*) I'm sorry for not respecting your privacy.

KATIE – Sorry, Amelia, for making fun of you.

MARIA – Are we still friends?

AMELIA – As long as you don't read my diary again!

KATIE and MARIA – It's a deal. (*Girls exit together.*)

RYAN – (*stands and confides in the HRDs.*) I read my older sister's diary all the time. I guess I shouldn't, eh?

HRD #1 – Right! And it would also be a good idea if you didn't listen-in on her telephone conversations.

RYAN – Hmm…, no eavesdropping?

HRD #1 and #2 – **No eavesdropping**!

RYAN – Okay.

(*HRDs cheer, give Ryan a high five, and the three exit.*)

| Human Rights for everyone | Not just a chosen few | Each person is important | Including me and you! |

SKIT 5 — FREEDOM OF OPINION AND EXPRESSION (AND THE IMPORTANCE OF INDIVIDUAL RIGHTS)

Everyone has the right to freedom of opinion and expression.

PARTS: (8+) – Mr. Clark, Patrick, Annie, 2 Human Rights Defenders (HRDs), 3 noisy students who sit in the front row, and remaining students.

SCENE: Students chat while teacher Mr. Clark completes the milk and pizza orders.

MR. CLARK – (*with authority*) Enough of that noise! Stop the chatter and get to work. *(Mr. Clark continues working at his desk. Three students in the front row still chat.)* You will **all** stay in at recess!

PATRICK – But Mr. Clark, some of us weren't talking. Why do we **all** have to stay in?

ANNIE – (*pipes up*) Yes, that doesn't seem fair!

MR. CLARK – (*turns toward Annie*) I don't want to hear another word about it!

HRD #1 and #2 – *(run into the scene, shouting)* FREEZE! (*Group freezes,*) *(HRDs start rapping.)* **Human Rights for everyone, not just a chosen few. Each person is important, including me and you!**

HRD #1 – It's not fair when a group is punished for the bad behaviour of a few.

HRD #2 – And all people have a right to **politely** express their own opinions. UNFREEZE! *(HRDs freeze.)*

MR. CLARK – You know, you're right. And thank you for pointing that out, Patrick. You three in the front row, who continued talking after I asked for quiet, will stay in at recess.

ANNIE – Mr. Clark, can the rest of us go outside?

MR. CLARK – Yes, you may.
   (Remaining students cheer quietly as they exit. HRDs cheer, give Mr. Clark a high five, and exit.)

| Human Rights for everyone | Not just a chosen few | Each person is important | Including me and you! |

SKIT 6 — FREEDOM FROM SLAVERY

No one shall be held in slavery.

PARTS: (4) – Craig, Mrs. Kielburger (Craig's mother), and 2 Human Rights Defenders (HRDs).

SCENE: Craig's mother is in the kitchen, preparing school lunches. Craig comes running in, picks up a bowl of cereal and starts eating.

NOTE: This is a true story of Canadian Craig Kielburger, who in 1995, at the age of 12, became a human rights champion.

MRS. KIELBURGER – (*points to the newspaper on the chair*)
   The newspaper's here, Craig.

CRAIG – Oh, great! I want to read the comics before I leave for school.
   (*Craig stares at the front page.*)

MRS. KIELBURGER – Craig, what's the matter?

CRAIG – (*reads headline aloud*) "Battled Child Labor Boy, 12, Murdered." He's the same age that I am! His name is Iqbal Masih and he's from Pakistan.

MRS. KIELBURGER – (*looks over Craig's shoulder and reads the article*) "When Iqbal Masih was four, his parents sold him into slavery for less than $16.00. For the next six years, he remained shackled to a carpet-weaving-loom most of the time, tying tiny knots hour after hour." (*sighs*) That's terrible! (*returns to making lunches*)

CRAIG – Mom, listen to this. It says that he was freed when he was twelve and travelled the world, crusading against child labour. Do you think that's why he was killed?

MRS. KIELBURGER – Yes, most likely.

CRAIG – What **is** child labour?

MRS. KIELBURGER – Why don't you look it up in the school library today. Maybe they'll have some information that will help.